"Orders were given to leave Allied fighters alone and concentrate on the bombers. This command led to a vicious spiral of disaster. The Luftwaffe concentrated on the bombers and were shot down by Allied fighters. The American fighters learned that they were safe against attack and became bolder and more effective. The Luftwaffe headed for bomber formations which supposedly were not escorted, but you ran into fighters anyway and in the end they were all over the place. The Luftwaffe developed an inferiority complex which got worse each day, but the High Command would not relax its order."

Oberst Johannes Kogler, Kommodore, Jagdgeschwader 6

'Imminent Danger West'

In March 1944, the *Luftwaffe* in north-west Europe was under the command of two *Luftflotten* which assumed ultimate responsibility for all German air power in the *Reich* and the occupied territories in the West. In terms of single-engined day fighters, *Luftflotte Reich*, with its headquarters at Dahlem in Berlin under the command of *Generaloberst* Hans-Jürgen Stumpff, marshalled those units engaged in the defence of the *Reich* – the *Reichsverteidigung* – based throughout Germany, Denmark, a part of Holland and Austria, while *Luftflotte* 3 under *Generalfeldmarschall* Hugo Sperrle, based in Paris, commanded the day fighter units based in France, Belgium and the rest of Holland.

LEFT: Generalfeldmarschall Hugo Sperrle, commander of Luftflotte 3, visiting an anti-shipping bomber unit at Istres. Sperrle was held responsible for the Luftwaffe's failure to repel the Allies in Normandy and on 19 August 1944, two days after the headquarters staff of Luftflotte 3 withdrew from Paris, Hitler ordered that he be replaced. Almost immediately, Sperrle issued an order of the day announcing his decision to surrender his post and thanked all members of the Luftflotte for their loyal co-operation. Sperrle then withdrew into civilian life and lived on the shores of a lake near Munich. He was succeeded as commander of Luftflotte 3 by Generaloberst Otto Dessloch, who in turn was displaced when Luftflotte 3 became Luftflotten Kommando West and was succeeded by Generalleutnant Alexander Holle. Although Sperrle was held responsible for Luftflotte 3's ineffectual performance in Normandy, the superiority of the Allied air forces was such that no matter what measures the Luftflotte may have taken, it was powerless to change the course of events.

Subordinate to each of the two *Luftflotten* was a *Jagdkorps* responsible for controlling day fighter tactical deployment in each *Luftflotte*. The I. *Jagdkorps*, under *Generalleutnant* Josef Schmid, managed those units of *Luftflotte Reich* engaged in the *Reichsverteidigung*, though it also occasionally directed units in parts of Holland and Belgium when necessary. The *Korps* was based at Zeist/Driebergen in Holland until 13 March when it relocated to Braunschweig-Querem.

The II. *Jagdkorps*, commanded by *Generalmajor* Werner Junck, a respected former First World War fighter pilot, was based at Chantilly, north of Paris, and controlled those units defending France and the Low Countries.

Reporting to the *Jagdkorps*, was a network of *Jagddivisionen* (Fighter Divisions) which directed regional day-to-day fighter operations and to which the *Jafü* – *Jagdflieger-führer* or local fighter commanders – reported.

Throughout March and in generally adverse weather conditions, the day fighters of both *Jagdkorps* fought a bitter battle of attrition as they defended Berlin and other central German targets from the US Eighth Air Force whose heavy bombers now relentlessly pounded the capital accompanied by increasing numbers of P-51 Mustang, P-47 Thunderbolt and P-38 Lightning escort fighters (see *Jagdwaffe* Volume Five, Section One). By this stage of the air war over Europe, the *Jagdwaffe* was outnumbered, outgunned and undertrained. In March, the *Luftwaffe* wrote off 56.4 per cent of the single-engined fighters available to it at the beginning of the month, while losses in fighter pilots amounted to 22 per cent of the strength available at the end of February.

LEFT: Hptm. Detlev Rohwer, the Kommandeur of II./JG 3, engaged P-51s escorting bombers to Braunschweig on 29 March but his Bf 109 G-6 was damaged in the ensuing combat. He made an emergency landing near Mettingen but was strafed on the ground by Allied fighters and severely wounded. He died the next day following the amputation of a leg. Rohwer had served with distinction during the 1940 battles against the RAF and had shot down three enemy fighters over England on 6 June of that year. He had been awarded the Ritterkreuz in October 1941 and went on to score a further 29 victories on the Russian Front with 2./JG 3. His final score stood at 38.

Within that number were several virtually irreplaceable formation leaders and *Experten*. JG 3, for example, lost the *Kommandeur* of its II. *Gruppe*, 27-year-old *Hptm*. Detlev Rohwer, when he was wounded on 29 March and died the following day.

JG 2, one of the two *Jagdgeschwader* operating in France under 4. *Jagddivision*, suffered particularly badly at this time when it lost its recently appointed *Kommodore, Major* Kurt Ubben. He had taken over command of the *Richthofen Geschwader* following the loss of *Obstlt*. Egon Mayer to American fighters in March – a month during which JG 2 had lost three *Staffelkapitäne*, all of them to P-47s. On 27 April, Ubben, formerly *Gruppenkommandeur* of III./JG 77 in Rumania, was also attacked by P-47s west of Reims during his third mission of the day. Though the veteran of the Russian Front and North Africa and 110-victory *Experte* who held the Oak Leaves to the *Ritterkreuz* managed to bale out of his Fw 190 A-8, his parachute failed to open. Also in April, the *Geschwader* lost another *Staffelkapitän* in combat with Allied fighters.

Nevertheless, the *Luftwaffe* continued to fight back. The Eighth Air Force lost 349 bombers in March 1944. *Generalleutnant* Schmid wrote that: '... *the striking power of the few remaining daylight fighter units assigned to the Reichsverteidigung remained unbroken. Whenever weather conditions permitted the concentrated employment in close combat formation in a single area, noteworthy success was achieved in bringing down enemy aircraft and in keeping our own losses to a reasonable limit. The success of our defensive operations over Berlin on 6 and 8 March gave ample evidence of the fighting morale of our fighter pilots and of their ability to execute effective combat despite the technical inferiority of their aircraft... If the Reichsverteidigung had 1,000 to 1,200 fighters available, it would doubtless have been in a position to alter the air situation, at least by day, in Germany's favour within a very short period of time, assuming of course, that there was no appreciable increase in American fighters.'*

BELOW AND BELOW RIGHT: An Fw 190 A-7 of the Gruppenstab of I./JG 11 being rearmed and refuelled at Rotenburg in March 1944. This aircraft was sometimes flown by Lt. Hans Schrangl who was credited with at least 14 victories.

ABOVE: After flying operations as a Zerstörer pilot, Rolf-Günther Hermichen transferred to fighters in November 1941 and joined III./JG 26 as an Oberleutnant. On 16 October, after acting as temporary Kommandeur of this Gruppe, Major Hermichen was given command of I./JG 11. By this time, Hermichen had already accumulated 41 victories and had become very successful against four-engined bombers so that, on 26 March 1944, with 61 victories, he received the Knight's Cross. His final total on 24 April 1944 was 64 victories, of which 26 were four-engined bombers. Subsequently, Major Hermichen commanded the fighter training Gruppe II./JG 104 and was awarded the Oak Leaves in February 1945. In this photograph, Hermichen is seen (right) with Major Hermann Graf, who was the Kommodore of JG 11 from 11 November 1943 to 29 March 1944.

I. *Jagdkorps* calculated that a comparison of strengths in March showed that the total number of American fighters and bombers outnumbered the single- and twin-engined fighters of I. *Jagdkorps* by a ratio of 7·5:1 whereas, in April, the same calculation had reduced to 4·5:1. Similarly, in terms of fighters alone, US strength compared with that of I. *Jagdkorps* was in the ratio of 3·6:1 in March, but had reduced to 2·2:1 in April.

Throughout April, the American bomber offensive ground on, targeting aircraft production plants in central and southern Germany, while US Eighth Air Force fighter escorts as well as tactical fighters of the US Ninth Air Force began to strafe German airfields. No airspace was safe and on the 8th, two experienced unit leaders were lost. Just after 13.45 hrs, *Oblt.* Josef Zwernemann, *Staffelkapitän* of

ABOVE: An Fw 190 A-7/R2, 'Yellow 5', W.Nr. 643910, of 6./JG 1 taking off from Störmede on 29 March to intercept a US bomber formation. On this date, six of the Gruppe's pilots were killed.

1./JG 11, attacked and shot down one of the 190 B-24s of the 2nd Bomb Division attacking Braunschweig. One minute later, east of Salzwedel, he claimed a P-51 escort fighter. A short while after that however, his Fw 190 A-7 was hit during an air battle with P-51s near Gardelegen. Baling out, he was reported to have been machine-gunned by an American fighter as he hung from his parachute. Zwernemann, was one of three pilots lost from 1./JG 11 that day; he held the Oak Leaves to the *Ritterkreuz* and was also a recipient of the *Ehrenpokal*. He had flown 600 missions and had been credited with 126 aerial victories. At 15.45 hrs, *Oblt.* Karl Willius, *Staffelkapitän* of 2./JG 26 and another veteran of the *Kanalfront* and the battles over England, was shot down by P-47s of the 361st FG following a head-on attack against the same stream of B-24s which Zwernemann had attacked. Willius' Fw 190 A-8 was seen to spin into the ground and explode. His *Ritterkreuz* was awarded posthumously and 11 of his 48 victories were *Viermots*.

From JG 3, *Oblt.* Otto Wessling, *Staffelkapitän* of 11. *Staffel*, was killed on 19 April when he made an emergency landing in his burning Bf 109 G-6 near Eschwege following operations against heavily escorted US bombers in the Göttingen/Kassel area. Wessling had been awarded the *Ritterkreuz* in September 1942 and posthumously received the Oak Leaves. He had accounted for 12 bombers in his total of 83 victories. Five days later, 1./JG 3 lost its commanding officer when *Lt.* Franz Schwaiger engaged large numbers of B-17s and their P-51 escorts north of Augsburg but was forced to make an emergency landing. He then climbed out of his Bf 109 G-5 but was strafed by P-51s and killed. Schwaiger

RIGHT: Feldmarschall Erwin Rommel was posted to France in December 1943 as commander of Army Group B and immediately began to strengthen the coastal defences. He is seen here, on the left, holding a field marshal's baton, probably in April 1944, during an inspection of JG 26. To the right of Rommel is Obstlt. Josef Priller, the Kommodore of JG 26.

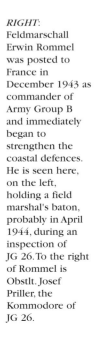

had been awarded the *Ritterkreuz* on 29 October 1942 and had been accredited with 67 victories, 56 of them scored on the Russian Front and four of them *Viermots*.

The endless low-level Allied attacks on German airfields, the constant alerts and general feeling of insecurity had also badly interrupted training. During April and May, 67 aircraft were shot down during training, transfer or travel flights over *Reich* territory.

But now a new and very serious threat emerged. Since April, *Generalmajor* Junck, the commander of II. *Jagdkorps* had repeatedly warned his immediate superiors at *Luftflotte* 3, as well as OKL, the *Luftwaffenführungsstab* and the *General der Jagdflieger*, of the nature of enemy air activity over France and Belgium, stating that the Invasion was at hand and calling for the allocation of appropriate forces and supplies.

Since February, Junck and his staff had been observing that the Allies were carrying out systematic and ever more regular day and night bombing attacks on railway yards and bridges, military bases, ammunition dumps, airfields and radars in northern France and areas south of the Seine. With this in mind, the Staff of II. *Jagdkorps* had, between February and June 1944, initiated its own studies of meteorological and tide conditions along the French coast in order to determine the location and periods at which a possible Allied invasion was most likely – or unlikely.

The *Korps* also made sure that its *Jagdgruppen* which, since the beginning of the year had been engaged in exhausting, almost daily defensive operations against US bomber incursions and Allied fighter sweeps over northern France, Belgium, Holland and western Germany, received some rest ahead of the predicted invasion. In April, I. and II./JG 26 had taken it in turns to fly to Cazeaux in the south of France where, ostensibly, they would receive training in attacking ground targets with WGr. 21 air-to-air mortars, but in reality they went there to enjoy brief spells of rest away from the demands of the Channel Front ahead of operations against an Allied landing. Likewise, in April, I./JG 2 returned from Italy to Aix-en-Provence, where it spent a month of rest and recuperation before moving to its base at Creil, north of Paris, in early May. On 14 May, III./JG 26 relocated from Étain to Nancy for a week of light training and the following day, II. *Gruppe* headed south once again to Mont de Marsan for more rest.

The following day, the 15th, the *General der Jagdflieger, Generalleutnant* Adolf Galland and *Generalleutnant* Schmid were ensconced behind closed doors with an argumentative Göring at Carinhall, the *Reichsmarschall's* country residence, where they held a heated discussion on the subject of fighters and fighter personnel. Galland reported depressing average daily operational loss rates for the month of April – 38 per cent in the area of *Luftflotte Reich*; 24 per cent in *Luftflotte* 3; 18.2 per cent in *Luftflotte* 2; 12 per cent in *Luftflotte* 5 and 11 per cent in *Luftlotten* 4, 6 and 1. In total, 489 fighter pilots had been lost in April, while reinforcements amounted to only 396. To rectify this situation, Galland proposed that any fighter pilot serving in a staff position should be withdrawn if considered still fit for flying, that 80-100 flying instructors as well as some night fighter pilots be sent to the *Jagdwaffe*, and that two *Jagdgruppen* be brought back from the East and retrained for operations in the *Reichsverteidigung*. Göring reluctantly agreed and promptly issued orders for II./JG 5 and IV./JG 54 to transfer. However, when Galland requested that the Fw 190-equipped ground-attack unit II./SG 2 be passed over to the *Jagdwaffe*, Göring refused. Galland argued that in this *Gruppe*, 11 pilots were known to have accumulated between five and 90 victories each – better scores than many fighter pilots.

ABOVE:
Oblt. Otto Wessling, Staffelkapitän of 11./JG 3 was killed in combat with US fighters near Eschwege on 19 April 1944.

RIGHT: A Bf 109 G-6 photographed just before taking off from Lille-Nord in March or April 1944. This particular machine, 'Black 22', was flown by Major Klaus Mietusch, the Kommandeur of III./JG 26 from 5 July 1943 until his death in action on 17 September 1944. Originally completed with a standard canopy, the aircraft has been retro-fitted with an Erla-Haub.

However, the *Reichsmarschall* would not be swayed, so Galland suggested that the *General der Schlachtflieger* should release any pilot with five or more aerial victories to his credit. Having consulted with *General der Flieger* Günther Korten, the *Luftwaffe* Chief of General Staff, Göring decided that any *Schlachtflieger* transferring to the *Jagdwaffe* should do so voluntarily but that the *Schlachtflieger* were not to be decisively weakened by this measure.

Galland pressed for the withdrawal of more *Jagdgruppen* from *Luftflotte* 3 in the West to the *Reich* for home defence, but again, Göring refused. Doggedly, Galland suggested that any fighter *Gruppenkommandeur* remaining absent from his command for 14 days owing to sickness or wounds, be replaced. Göring again refused, as such *Kommandeure* were too sparse to fritter away with unproductive disciplinary measures. However, Göring did concede to another request for a continuous withdrawal of *Jagdgruppen* from each *Jagddivision* for a period of eight days to four weeks to rest and re-equip, provided that the withdrawal of II./JG 5 and IV./JG 54 from the East proceeded swiftly.

Such measures highlighted how thin the so-called 'steel umbrella' over Germany and the West really was and that the stretched resources led to competition and friction between the commands. In a report written in November 1944, *Oberst* Mettig, the former Chief of Staff of II. *Jagdkorps*, let his thoughts on Galland's proposals for withdrawing *Luftflotte* 3's fighter assets to the Reich be known: '*The fighter forces available were utterly insufficient – up to the beginning of the Invasion, they comprised two Geschwader with a total operational strength of 60-80 aircraft... It was decided to send one Gruppe at a time from each Geschwader back to the Metz-Nancy area for training under more peaceful conditions... The suggestion that these units might more profitably be transferred to Bohemia or Silesia for training was turned down by the Luftwaffenführungsstab with the comments that a) no airfields were available and b) that the danger would exist of both Geschwader being incorporated into Luftgau Reich and therefore being lost to II. Jagdkorps.*'

ABOVE: 'White 17', a Bf 109 G-6 of 9./JG 26 at Lille-Nord, was flown by the *Staffelkapitän*, Hptm. Hans-Georg Dippel who had 19 victories. Dippel was killed in this machine on 8 May 1944 when the aircraft stalled and crashed while he was performing aerobatics at low speed over his airfield.

For his part, Josef Schmid had not been entirely lacking a sense of urgency or reality. He realised that a significant and successful interception of the Invasion could affect the course of the war and ordered the establishment of a dedicated 'Transfer Staff' within I. *Jagdkorps* – responsible for the bulk of the day fighters – whose task it would be to prepare for the transfer of flying units from the *Reichsverteidigung* into any possible invasion zone.

This staff had been quietly formed on 8 December 1943 under *Oberst* Otto von Lachemair, who had been *Kommandeur* of II./KG 55 at the start of the war and later *Kommandeur* of *Flugzeugführerschule* A/B 114 before being transferred to the Staff of I. *Jagdkorps*. It was based at the *Korps* Headquarters and consisted of Lachemair, three assistants with the rank of *Hauptmann*, and a limited number of junior personnel, all of whom reported directly to Schmid. According to Lachemair: '*The preparations for the repulsion of an invasion were to be made in compliance with an ever increasing number of detailed directives issued by OKL and these were a considerable burden on I. Jagdkorps in the second half of 1943. In view of the decisive importance of a successful repulsion of an invasion on the overall conduct of the war and of the increased strain imposed on the staffs and units of the Reichsverteidigung by the intensity of the air war over the Reich, the Commander of the I. Jagdkorps decided to organise a 'Transfer Staff'.*'

In the summer of that year, Göring had devised a system of code words which, in the event of an Allied invasion, would trigger defensive measures organised by I. *Jagdkorps*. Transmission of the code words 'Imminent Danger North' signalled an invasion of Norway or Denmark, while 'Imminent Danger West' signalled a landing in the coastal areas of Holland, Belgium or western France. 'Imminent Danger South' signalled an invasion in southern France.

Provisional schedules were drawn up taking into account all possible eventualities and rapid lines of communication were established between the Transfer Staff and the staffs of the respective *Jagdkorps*, *Jagddivisionen* and *Luftgau* in the areas of potential risk. Attempts were made to train the home defence units in bombing and strafing of ground and water-borne targets and studies were made into tidal and meteorological conditions along the French coast. More than 1,000 fighters were on stand-by in the *Reich*, but despite these extraordinary preparations, there were still certain weaknesses in these measures, for while Lachemair was able to write that '*Combat morale and bearing of the crews in the Reich defence were admirable...*', he also pointed out that in I. *Jagdkorps* the situation was such that '*...an understanding commander would not have been surprised to find low spirits and despondency.*'

Similarly, if Schmid had any intention of readily releasing any of his I. *Jagdkorps* units for deployment to repel an anticipated invasion in the West, he certainly gave no indication of it. At the end of March 1944, Schmid noted that: '*... despite the growing numerical superiority of the American forces, there had been no change in the organisation or operation of the Reich air defence forces. There could be no increase in the strength of our daytime fighter units since the production of fighter aircraft had fallen far behind schedule as a result of the successful enemy attacks on our aircraft factories. For the same reason, no new units could be activated. There seemed to be no chance of withdrawing fighters from other fronts. The command organisation of the Reichsverteidigung had not been altered in any way, and thus no effective concentration of fighter strength was possible.*'

However, attempts were made to improve the fragmentation of the command structure. At 21.00 hrs on 31 March, a message clattered out of the teletype machines at the headquarters of I. and II. *Jagdkorps*. It was from *Luftflotte Reich* and read:

'*For the purpose of concentrating the Reichsverteidigung in the Reich as well as in the occupied western territories, the Reichsmarschall has issued the following orders:*

With immediate effect, 7. Jagddivision including Jafü Ostmark will be assigned to I. Jagdkorps. Thus I. Jagdkorps, subordinate to Luftflotte Reich assumes command of all fighter operations within the Reich and in particular, the fighter defence of southern and south-west Germany against enemy incursions from the south. Close contact will be maintained with Luftflotte 2.

The day fighter forces of Luftflotte 3 will be concentrated and employed in the sector of II. Jagdkorps for the defence of the occupied western territories, in particular those of the important supply and transportation centres as well as friendly ground organisations. These forces will be committed in the Reichsverteidigung only against such enemy forces intruding or leaving the Reich via south-west Belgium and France. Transfers of these units over longer distances into the Reich's territory will be avoided in future. The night fighter forces assigned to Luftflotte 3 will be assigned hitherto to Reich defence.

Particular attention is called for in the close cooperation between I. and II. Jagdkorps as well as between Luftflotte Reich and Luftflotte 3 by prompt communication of situation information and operational objectives. Special directives will be issued regarding signals communications and improvements in radar and fighter control systems as well as the possible transfer of the I. Jagdkorps command post.'

Under direct threat from the Allies in the West, Josef Schmid went to considerable lengths to arrange conferences at which he informed the commanders of home defence fighter units of the anti-invasion measures being taken. The creation of Lachemair's Transfer Staff had gone some way towards building a link between the *Luftwaffe's* fighter commands in France and those engaged in home defence. Its various functions included the preparation of a fast-response schedule; the sufficient additional training of fighter units in bombing and strafing attacks on ground and water-borne targets; overseeing the re-equipping of aircraft as required in the event of an invasion; the preparation for transfer of individual flying units and the motorised elements of the ground organisations.

For this purpose it was necessary to:
   a) ensure availability of additional equipment, ammunition and motor vehicles.
   b) reconnoitre and establish the receiving airfields in co-operation with their command staffs.
   c) establish air and land transfer routes and ensure adequate supplies for the units during their transfers and immediately upon arrival at receiving airfields.

However, Lachemair and his staff found their job difficult, as Schmid explained:

'*In itself, preparation for the transfer of flying units from the Reich to France and for the conversion of these units' role and equipment to another type of employment was nothing unusual. But it was the conditions existing during the period of preparation that were unusual.*'

'*The Reich defence fighter units were almost daily engaged in fierce combat against Allied air attacks. They sustained heavy losses and their operations absorbed commanders and their pilots to such an extent that anything not regarded as essentially necessary for the task in hand was liable to be classed of secondary importance. The great number of written orders, supplements and amendments issued by OKL as a result of the constantly changing overall situation in the Reichsverteidigung not only impaired the transfer operation, but caused much confusion in the staff and units of the heavily strained home air defence... An officer responsible for preparation of the transfer operation was appointed in each Jagddivision, Jagdgeschwader, Jagdgruppe and Staffel. One officer from the Transfer Staff remained at I. Jagdkorps headquarters to receive orders, to receive and forward reports and to receive and answer inquiries related to the 'Imminent Danger' policy. However, the head of the staff and two of its officers were constantly on the move in aircraft or by car offering assistance to the units and clarifying problems. This activity showed its results especially in respect to the speeding up of additional supplies of ammunition and other materiel and vehicles effected in close association with the supply agencies of Luftflotte Reich and I. Jagdkorps headquarters.'*

At the end of March 1944, Lachemair reported to Schmid advising that preparations for the issuing of an 'Imminent Danger' code word had been completed and that the time required from the moment the code word was issued by *Korps* headquarters to the time the *Jagdgruppen* would be ready for transfer would be approximately two hours.

On 1 April 1944, Lachemair confirmed that the following measures were in place:
  a) Unit commanders and their staffs had been briefed on the concept of 'Imminent Danger'
  b) Optimum availability of equipment, arms, ammunition and vehicles for conversion and transfer purposes had been organised.
  c) Training for defensive action over an invasion front was complete, despite the heavy strain imposed by the demands of *Reich* defence.
  d) Thorough briefings at the airfields in the possible invasion zones and the routes to be used in the eventuality of a sudden transfer had been carried out.
  e) Supply chains had been established in case of transfer.
  f) Lines of communication had been established with command staffs in possible invasion zones down to and including airfield commands at receiving airfields.

On 13 May 1944, following operational experiences in Italy, the OKL Operations Staff issued a Tactical Directive in which it predicted the need for fighter units to adapt to operational demands when confronted with '*.... an enemy superior both in numbers and quality as will surely be the case in a landing in the West. In case of an enemy landing, the use of bomb-carrying fighters to support ground-attack units will become necessary. Since time is short, suitable training for fighter units in ground-attack missions is to be undertaken. To maintain operational readiness, fighter units will undertake this additional training on operational airfields.'*

OKL envisaged the need for both Fw 190s and Bf 109s to make close-formation diving attacks in *Gruppe* and *Staffel* strength with bombs against ships in the landing area followed where possible by strafing attacks, again in *Staffel* strength. In a summary of his mission, Lachemair concluded:

'*Upon orders of the I. Jagdkorps, I inspected all fighter units in the area of the Reichsverteidigung during the months preceding D-Day... Combat morale and bearing of the men in the Reichsverteidigung were admirable. This did not only apply to the flight crews, but was also true of the technical ground personnel. There were only two sources from which the fighter units could gather strength to keep up their unique attitude and these were firstly, their recognition of the necessity of their fight for their bleeding homeland and their commitment in combat, which was beyond any reproach; secondly, the confidence in their commanders up to their commanding general who demanded total commitment in combat, but who also appreciated their accomplishments and protected their honour as soldiers. At that time there was not much to inspire the heart of a young soldier with enthusiasm. The fighting had become more unequal from day to day, the numerical superiority of the attackers was overwhelming, the homeland more and more damaged, the successes obtained were necessarily more and more limited, confidence had decreased steadily, and finally, the disgraceful reproaches by the German High Command were the worst enemy of all.'*

Despite the reinforcement of *Reich* defence with the arrival during May of II./JG 5 and IV./JG 54 in accordance with Göring's and Galland's earlier discussions, it was a black month for losses of skilled pilots and formation leaders. On the 8th, the Eighth Air Force struck at Berlin and Braunschweig with a force of nearly 800 bombers escorted by more than 700 fighters. *Lt.* Leopold Münster, *Staffelkapitän* of 5./JG 3 was scrambled along with the rest of II./JG 3 from Sachau at 08.42 hrs. Just after 10.00 hrs, west of Braunschweig, his unit encountered B-17s and the 24-year-old *Ritterkreuzträger* quickly claimed one of these, followed by a B-24 a little later in a second action in the Hildesheim area. Unfortunately, Münster's Bf 109 G-6 was too close to its target as it exploded under the force of his attack and the German pilot was killed in the blast over Wöllersheim. A veteran of the Mediterranean and Russian Fronts, he had been credited with 95 victories including 15 *Viermots*.

BELOW: Shortly before the Allies launched Operation 'Overlord', Oblt. Horst Carganico, Kommandeur of I./JG 5, was killed. His aircraft was damaged during an engagement with US bombers on 27 May 1945 and crashed into high tension wires while Carganico was attempting a forced landing. Carganico had more than 60 victories and had been awarded the Ritterkreuz in September 1941.

*THIS PAGE:*This Fw 190 A-8, seen here with a Luftwaffe war correspondent in the fuselage, was flown by Ofhr. Wolfgang Rose of 4./JG 26. Lt. Helmut Menge, another pilot of 4. Staffel, disappeared during an early-morning mission over the Allied beachhead while flying this aircraft on 10 June 1944. Ofhr. Rose himself was killed when he was shot down by US fighters on 27 June.

Focke-Wulf Fw 190 A-8 'Blue 10' flown by Ofhr. Wolfgang Rose of 4./JG 26, Spring 1944
Ofhr. Rose's 'Blue 10' was finished in a standard 74/75/76 camouflage scheme with a yellow panel under the nose and a yellow rudder. The use of blue as a Staffel colour began in 1943 when the Geschwader was expanded to twelve Staffeln and was used by the 4., 8., and 12. Staffeln from March 1944 to March 1945.

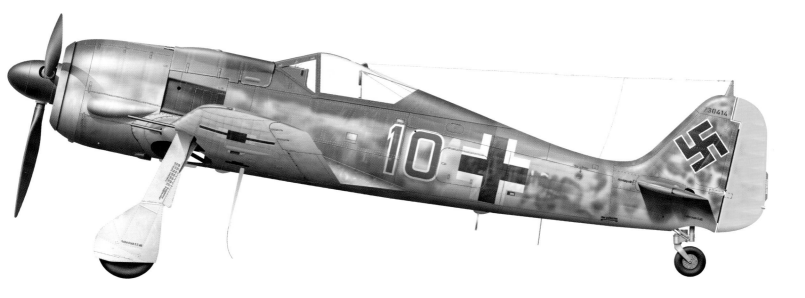

On 27 May, *Major* Horst Carganico, the *Gruppenkommandeur* of I./JG 5 was killed in France when his Bf 109 G-5 crashed at Chevry, near St. Dizier as he was making an emergency landing. His unit had just engaged a formation of B-17s and his machine had taken hits from the bombers' defensive fire. Carganico, the son of a *Luftwaffe* general, was a 60-victory *Experte* and *Ritterkreuzträger* who had previously flown with JG 77 over Norway, England and Russia. But perhaps the greatest blow of all had occurred on 11 May when the Eighth Air Force attacked marshalling yards in north-eastern France, Belgium and Luxembourg. Nearly 900 bombers took part, and the fighter escort flew over 1,000 sorties. At Paderborn, the Bf 109 Gs of *Stab* and III./JG 1 took off in the afternoon, with the *Geschwaderkommodore*, *Oberst* Walter Oesau, a veteran of the Spanish Civil War and a 123-victory *Experte* who wore the *Ritterkreuz* with *Eichenlaube* and *Schwerten*, leading three aircraft of the *Stabsschwarm*. They were followed by the Bf 109 G-6s of III./JG 1, led by *Major* Hartmann Grasser. The *Stabsschwarm* was diving towards the bombers when it was bounced by American fighters and Oesau was engaged by five enemy aircraft. His wingmen, themselves fully occupied by the encounter, could do nothing to help. Attempting to escape, Oesau progressively lost height. *Ofw.* Leo Schuhmacher of II./JG 1 recalled: "*Several times I had said to Oesau that the Fw 190 was better than the Bf 109, but being an old 109 pilot, he preferred it. On 11 May, [Heinz] Bär [Gruppenkommandeur of II./JG 1] remained on the ground because of technical problems and Oesau led the formation totalling 30 aircraft. At high altitude we spotted the enemy fighters and Oesau ordered me over the radio to take II. Gruppe with me. As I was later told by his wingman, a young Oberfähnrich, Oesau was attacked by P-51s which forced him into a turning dogfight. Each turn became tighter, and the Bf 109 slowed down, more so than his adversaries. Oesau was probably shot down near the ground. I saw Oesau's body; the whole left side of him appeared to have been hit by a burst. Thus wounded, he no doubt tried to carry out a makeshift landing.*"

The remains of Oesau's Bf 109 G-6 were found several kilometres from St. Vith in Belgium. His body was found not far away. It had been thrown clear on impact. Several years after the war, *Major* Grasser, an *Eichenlaubträger* with close on 100 victories gained in both the East and West and who had just taken over III./JG 1, also commented on Oesau's loss: "*At that time, Oesau was physically and mentally exhausted. The German fighter pilots, like their officers, had to fight right through the war, without respite. I consider it a grave error on the part of our High Command. I personally took part in the combat when Oesau was lost. Alone, chased by Lightnings and Mustangs, he had no chance of escaping. Neither did we. It was in this way that we lost the majority of the best among us.*"

In a sad twist of fate, several hours after Oesau's disappearance, a letter signed by Galland arrived at the unit's *Stab*. It was an order posting Oesau to Galland's headquarters staff, but by then it was too late. All that could be done was to honour the fallen hero and, henceforth, the premier fighter unit would be known as *Jagdgeschwader* 1 'Oesau.'

Oesau's loss was irreplaceable and his leadership and experience – and those of the other *Experten* lost in the spring of 1944 – would be sorely felt by the *Jagdwaffe* during the following, critical weeks.

LEFT: Major Heinz Bär, the Kommandeur of II./JG 1, in the cockpit of his Fw 190 A-7 'Red 23' photographed in the evening of 22 April 1944 upon his return to the Gruppe's base at Störmede after destroying a Liberator as his 200th victory. As 'Red 23' was Bär's reserve machine, the victory marking was applied to his other Fw 190 A-7, 'Red 13'.

LEFT: This Bf 109 G-14 belonged to 9./JG 26 and was probably photographed at Lille-Nord a few weeks before the Allied Invasion of France which was given the code name 'Operation Overlord' and known to the German command as 'Imminent Danger West'. This aircraft, which shows very little wear and tear and has no exhaust staining along the fuselage, was fitted with a tall tail unit but has retained the original canopy.

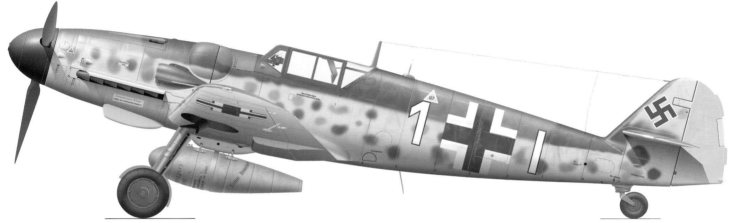

Messerschmitt Bf 109 G-14 'White 1' of 9./JG 26, 1944
This aircraft was camouflaged in the typical three-tone grey scheme comprising the colours 74/75/76 and had a yellow rudder and yellow panel under the nose. The spinner was a plain, semi-gloss black, and the fuselage had an area forward of the windscreen which had evidently been repainted with 75.

RIGHT: Probably also photographed at Lille-Nord at the same time was this Bf 109 G-6 which is believed to have carried the tactical number 'White 18'. Note that the rear canopy framing appears to be natural metal.

ABOVE: Hptm. Karl-Heinz Weber, seen here on the right, flew with JG 51 in the East where he became Staffelkapitän of 7./JG 51. In late May 1944, at which time Weber had 136 victories, 7./JG 51 was transferred to the Western Front to reinforce JG 1 in the Defence of the Reich. On 3 June, Weber was appointed Kommandeur of III./JG 1 but on the 7th, while flying his first mission over the Invasion Front, he was shot down and killed, apparently by Mustangs, near Caen. He was posthumously awarded the Eichenlaub on 20 July.

LEFT AND BELOW: A Bf 109 G-6 of 11./JG 26 taxiing past some locally recruited construction workers on a forward airfield in the West in the spring of 1944. The aircraft is finished in the then still standard 74/75/76 scheme and has the underside of the engine cowling painted yellow.

RIGHT: An Fw 190 A-7 of II./JG 26 being manoeuvred into its dispersal beneath the trees at Boissy-le-Bois in late June 1944. This airfield, located on farmland between Beauvais and Paris, remained undetected by the Allies for some weeks following the Invasion.

ABOVE AND RIGHT: An Fw 190 A-8/R6 of Stab JG 26 being loaded with a 21 cm mortar round. This weapon had originally been introduced in 1943 as a means of attacking bomber formations. Although the results of a direct hit were devastating and even blast from a near miss was sufficient to break up a bomber formation, they were not as effective as had been hoped. Apart from the tendency of German pilots to fire from too great a range, the launch tubes had a detrimental effect on the aircraft's performance which resulted in units being reluctant to employ them in areas where bombers were accompanied by a fighter escort. When, in the summer of 1944, the military situation in the West demanded that they be reintroduced, they were used during strafing attacks against Allied ground forces as well as against bomber formations.

ABOVE: A close-up view of a WGr 21 cm mortar tube showing attachment points and electrical wiring outlets.

ABOVE: Fw 190s of 7./JG 26 in flight in early May 1944. The aircraft nearest the camera is an Fw 190 A-7, 'Brown 4', which was flown by the Staffelkapitän, Oblt. Waldemar Radener. The rudder of this machine is marked with 21 victory bars, the most recent representing a B-24 of the 487th Bomb Group which Radener attacked on 11 May. On that occasion he was flying an A-8 with the tactical number 'Brown 2', but soon collided with another B-24 and baled out with minor injuries. The A-7 shown here is therefore his replacement aircraft. At the end of January, Radener became Kommandeur of II./JG 26 and led this Gruppe until 22 February when he transferred to command II./JG 300. He was still serving with this Gruppe when he was awarded the Ritterkreuz on 12 March, although this was largely in respect of his achievements while with II./JG 26. Radener survived the war with 37 victories and subsequently joined the Bundesluftwaffe, only to be killed in a flying accident in 1957.

Focke-Wulf Fw 190 A-7 'Brown 4' flown by Oblt. Waldemar Radener, Staffelkapitän of 7./JG 26, early May 1944
After March 1944, 7./JG 26 was the only Staffel of the Geschwader to use brown as a Staffel colour and this remained in use for a year. Otherwise, the external appearance of this machine is typical of the period with camouflage consisting of a 74/75/76 scheme. The yellow rudder is marked with 21 victory bars in black.

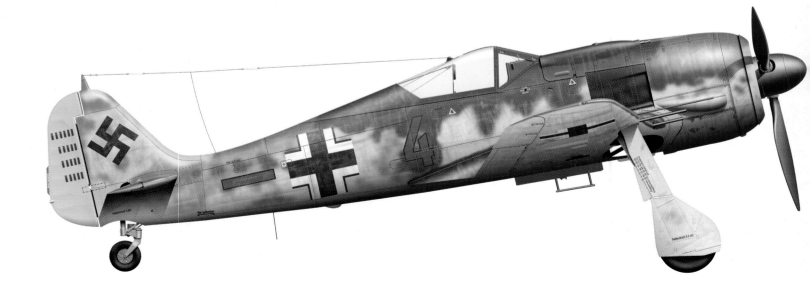

LEFT: Until the Allied landings in France, the bulk of the German fighter force was committed to Reich Defence and on 5 June 1944, Luftflotte 3, which was responsible for aerial operations in repelling the Invasion, possessed a total single-engined fighter force of not more than 170 aircraft. However, under a long-standing contingency plan to send in reinforcements on a major scale, commencing on 6 June, the Luftwaffe began to dispatch almost its entire home defence single-seat fighter force to airfields in France. By 10 June, fifteen Gruppen of fighters with some 300 aircraft, were flown in from Germany where only three Gruppen of single-seat fighters – two from JG 300 and one from JG 301 – remained to mount a token defence of the homeland. Once in France, a considerable proportion of the aircraft were fitted with bomb racks to enable them to operate as fighter-bombers in support of ground forces. One such unit previously engaged in Reich Defence was IV.(Sturm)/JG 3, and here, the Gruppe's armourers are preparing to load an SC 250 bomb onto one of the unit's Fw 190 A-8/R2 aircraft. Just visible on the side of the canopy is the panel of armoured glass added to provide the pilot with additional protection.

RIGHT: A ground-to-air view of a Bf 109 of III./JG 1 flying over the airfield at La Fère in July 1944. This aircraft is believed to be a G-6 W.Nr. 163836 of 9.Staffel with the tactical number 'Yellow 4'.

RIGHT:
Ofw. Friedrich Zander of the Stab of III./JG 1 after landing at La Fère following a sortie in July 1944. Just visible on the far right of the picture is the aircraft's tactical number, 'Blue 22'. Killed in an air battle near Bastogne on 26 December 1944, Zander was one of the Gruppe's longest-serving pilots and, with 38 victories, one of its most successful.

LEFT: A Bf 109 G-6 of 7./JG 1 landing at La Fère, probably in July 1944. The aircraft on the ground, 'White 9', also belonged to the same Staffel.

ABOVE: 'Yellow 2', a heavily exhaust-stained Bf 109 G-14 of 9./JG 1, landing at La Fère in July 1944. The aircraft has an Erla canopy and tall tail unit, and clearly visible on the fin is the W.Nr. 413553.

BELOW: 'White 9' of 7./JG 1 being towed by a lorry on the airfield at La Fère. Although this scene might suggest that there was a shortage of aviation fuel, in fact increased production and strict economy measures had ensured that by the summer of 1944 a stock of some 540,000 tons was at the disposal of the Luftwaffe. Approximately 20,000 tons of fuel, sufficient for a month of intensive operations, was available in France and the Low Countries.

Mass against Mass 1 – *Gefechtsverbände*

On 2 April 1944, following a series of earlier attempts which had to be aborted on account of the weather, the US Fifteenth Air Force in Italy sent nearly 450 B-17s and B-24s to the ball-bearing and Daimler aircraft components plants at Steyr in Austria. The bombs were to be released through cloud and the bombers were escorted by P-38s and P-47s.

In response, I. *Jagdkorps* deployed 226 fighters from units of 3. *Jagddivision* from the Frankfurt area towards Wels and units of 7. *Jagddivision* based in Bavaria towards Passau and Salzburg, and from Vienna towards the Graz area. One such unit operating under the command of 7. *Jagddivision* was IV./JG 27 based at Graz-Thalerhof under *Hptm*. Otto Meyer. In a typical action led by Meyer, the *Gruppe's* Bf 109 G-6s were ordered to intercept the American formation as it approached from the direction of Linz. They made contact with the bombers shortly after 10.30 hrs in the area between Graz and Klagenfurt. At a height of 7,000 metres, IV./JG 27 manoeuvred for a rear attack and in a short, intense air battle, the Bf 109s swept in from behind and below, opening fire with their MG 151/20 cannon from 200 metres. In a series of attacks lasting 15 minutes, the *Gruppe* claimed four *Abschüsse* and three *Herausschüsse*. *Hptm*. Meyer claimed two of the *Herausschüsse* for his 13th and 14th victories, while at 10.47 hrs, *Fw*. Werner Döring of 12./JG 27 flying 'Yellow 6', who was leading a *Schwarm* of Bf 109s comprising *Uffz*. Otto Kühn as his wingman with the other *Rotte* led by *Fw*. Rudolf Philipp, targeted the rearmost flight of Liberators of the last box. Döring selected one bomber and scored hits on the fuselage and left wing. The B-24 fell away from its formation and the German pilots watched as it passed away and below them trailing thick smoke. Later that day, *Hptm*. Meyer and *Lt*. Franz Stigler, *Staffelkapitän* of 12./JG 27 approved Döring's claim for a *Herausschuss*.

LEFT: In order to knock down four-engined bombers, the weight of German fighter armament was increased, as shown on this Bf 109 G-6 with 20 mm MG 151 cannon in the underwing gondolas. However, as this placed German single-engined fighters at a severe disadvantage when engaged by Allied escort fighters, the Luftwaffe introduced the concept of engaging the bombers with heavily armed Sturmgruppe protected by an escort of lightly armed fighters.

Franz Stigler recalled that attacking bombers was a draining, dangerous process: "*B-24s suffered from* [a build up of] *fuel fumes in the fuselage and that was their weak point. We found that they were easier to shoot down because they burned. The B-17s took a lot more punishment. It was terrifying. I saw them in some cases with their tail fins torn in half, elevators missing, tail gun sections literally shot to pieces, ripped away, but they still flew. We found them a lot harder to bring down than the Liberators. The Liberators sometimes went up in flames right in front of you.*

"*Attacking bombers became a very mechanical, impersonal kind of warfare; one machine against another. That's why I always tried to count the parachutes. If you saw eight, nine or ten 'chutes come out safely, then you knew it was OK, you felt better about it. But when you flew through a formation, the B-17s couldn't miss you. If they did something was wrong. I never came back from attacking bombers without a hole somewhere in my aircraft.*"

Also in action against the Steyr attack on 2 April was III./JG 3 which put 17 Bf 109s into the air at 09.56 hrs led by *Lt*. Jürgen Hörschelmann. Assembling with aircraft of I./JG 5 over Passau at

7,000 metres, the Messerschmitts set course for Steyr and soon sighted B-17s of the 5th Bombardment Wing. As the *Gruppe* made its attack, American escort fighters intercepted and the unit immediately suffered two losses when one pilot was forced to bale out and the aircraft of *Uffz*. Alfred Damaschko was hit and was seen to plunge into cloud. Damaschko crashed to his death 40 kilometres south-east of Steyr. However, breaking through the fighter defence, the remaining fighters attacked the bombers and claimed five *Abschüsse* including one by *Lt*. Hörschelmann and one by *Lt*. Raimund Koch, each of whose claims represented their respective 14th victories. Nevertheless, the unit returned to Wörishofen missing three further aircraft which had crash-landed.

In summarising operations for April 1944, *Generalleutnant* Schmid stated that the main purpose of the *Jagdwaffe* units engaged in the *Reichsverteidigung* was to combat bombers and not to tackle fighters and win air superiority:

'*The daylight air warfare over the Reich with the increased American offensive action had brought about a psychological effect on all Luftwaffe command staffs and dominated them. Nowhere, at no command headquarters, neither at OKH, nor at OKL, nor on the staff of the General der Jagdflieger, nor at Luftflotte Reich, nor at the headquarters of I. Jagdkorps was an adequate plan under consideration for operations to gain air supremacy by a victorious fighter battle. The attention of all responsible commanders was focused on only one danger – the Flying Fortress and their bomb loads. The persistent demand for destroying American bombers by an incessant commitment of fighters originated with the Führer.*'

The principle of the '*Gefechtsverband*', or battle formation, a large composite formation of fighters, was being increasingly adopted by the Germans as a means with which to tackle mass with mass. In this regard, the *Gruppen* of JG 3 often flew into action alongside the heavily armed and armoured Fw 190 A-6s and A-7s of *Sturmstaffel* 1, the specialist close-range 'bomber killer' unit formed by *Major* Hans-Günter von Kornatzki the previous autumn.

On 8 April, fog prevented a large part of the US 1st Bombardment Division from taking off to attack its assigned target, the airfield at Oldenburg. The 3rd Bombardment Division despatched 255 B-17s to airfields across north-west Germany and the B-24 Liberators of the 2nd Bombardment Division headed for aircraft production plants at Braunschweig as well as Langenhagen airfield and other targets. The whole force was protected by 780 fighters. In response, a *Gefechtsverband* comprising *Sturmstaffel* 1 and *Stab*, I., II., and IV./JG 3 was scrambled to intercept the US raid north-west of Braunschweig. Launching a massed frontal attack over Fallersleben, a massive air battle commenced, the sky swirling with P-51s, P-38s, Bf 109s and Fw 190s as the bombers lumbered on with their bomb run.

The *Sturmstaffel* attacked a box of Liberators and within a matter of minutes had shot down four of them with *Uffz*. Kurt Röhrich claiming his fifth victory with *Lt*. Siegfried Müller and *Lt*. Richard Franz claiming their third victories. *Uffz*. Heinz Steffen was credited with a *Herausschuss*, also as his third victory. As *Lt*. Franz remembered:

"*After this mission, I had the opportunity to meet a crew member of the bomber I had shot down. I landed at Magdeburg airfield and met him there in the operations room. He was a lieutenant, his name was Andy and he was the only member of the crew who had survived the attack. We had a good talk and he presented me with his flying jacket – half leather and half silk with 24 previous missions written in ink on the silk part of the jacket, including the date and target. He told me that this was their last mission and that, had they returned, they would have been posted back to the States. But he also felt lucky to be alive. I had that jacket until the end of the war, when I was shot down for the last time on 25 April 1945 by a Russian fighter over Berlin.*"

The next day, over 400 USAAF *Viermots* escorted by 719 fighters attacked aircraft factories and airfields in north east Germany. A *Gefechtsverband* under the command of the *Ritterkreuzträger Major* Friedrich-Karl Müller and comprising *Sturmstaffel* 1 and IV./JG 3 was assembled over the Baltic coast near Rügen and the air battle began shortly before midday. IV./JG 3 accounted for seven *Viermots*, with *Oblt*. Otto Wessling scoring his 77th victory (although he would be killed in action ten days later) and *Lt*. Hans Iffland knocked down two for his sixth and seventh victories. *Sturmstaffel* 1 also claimed a bomber.

On the 11th, the Americans launched an all-out assault against centres of aircraft production in eastern Germany. A record-breaking force of 917 B-17s and B-24s was assembled to strike at the Focke-Wulf plants at Poznan and Sorau, the Junkers plants at Bernburg and Halberstadt, the Pommersche Motorenbau works at Stettin and Cottbus and various assembly plants at Oschersleben. This enormous

BELOW: A veteran of the Kanalkampf, North Africa and Italy, Major Friedrich-Karl Müller was awarded the Ritterkreuz in September 1941 on his 30th victory and was appointed Kommandeur of I./JG 3 in August 1942 before moving to I./JG 53 in November of that year. He was decorated with the Eichenlaube to the Ritterkreuz on 23 September 1942 upon scoring 100 victories. He went on to become deputy Kommodore of JG 53 the following autumn before returning to JG 3, first as Kommandeur of I. Gruppe, before being appointed Geschwader-kommodore on 11 April 1944. He was credited with a total of some 140 victories.

armada was protected by more than 800 fighters drawn from 13 fighter groups of the Eighth Air Force and four from the Ninth Air Force's Third Division, though with bomber resources stretched over such a wide range of deep penetration targets, even this escort was barely adequate and weather conditions had improved only marginally over those prevailing on the 9th.

In response, the I. *Jagdkorps* sent up a total of 432 single- and twin-engined fighters drawn from 1., 2. and 3. *Jagddivision*. *Sturmstaffel* 1 and IV./JG 3 received the *Alarmstart* order and took off from Salzwedel at 10.05 hrs and formed up into a *Gefechtsverband* with elements of various units drawn from 1. and 3. *Jagddivision*. The Americans were sighted some 40 minutes later between Braunschweig and Halberstadt. *Sturmstaffel* 1 separated from IV./JG 3, with the latter unit directing its attack against a combat box of B-17s, whilst the *Sturmstaffel* closed in on a formation of some 50 B-24 Liberators from the 2nd Bombardment Division in the Hildesheim area. For the Americans it was to be carnage, whilst the *Sturmstaffel* enjoyed its most successful action in its short-lived history. Five B-24s were either shot down or cut away from their formation in 60 seconds. IV./JG 3 claimed a staggering 23 B-17s shot down or severely damaged, including three by the redoubtable Otto Wessling who raised his score to 80 victories. JG 1 also gave a good account of itself, despite failing to form up with II./JG 27, and claimed 16 Viermots downed, while I. and III./JG 11 claimed 19.

In its Narrative of Operations, the Eighth Air Force reported on the combined attack: '... *the leading group on Oschersleben was not attacked until it reached the IP near Hildesheim where about 50 Fw 190s and Me 109s were seen. A number of enemy aircraft passed through the formation in ones and twos from 10 o'clock making unpressed attacks. The last combat wing on Oschersleben encountered about 25 Fw 190s and Me 109s which attacked aggressively just after the target. Enemy aircraft would come in three or four abreast or in a V formation from ahead or high and level.*'

The Eighth Air Force also concluded that the *Luftwaffe* had mounted '... *one of its most severe and well co-ordinated defences marked by skilful handling of a considerable number of twin-engined day fighters in the Stettin area and single-engine fighters in the Hannover-Oschersleben area.*'

Following this action, a few *Sturmjäger*, together with elements of IV./JG 3, joined up and flew in formation back to Salzwedel. Once landed, they quickly refuelled and rearmed for a second mission directed against the returning bombers. They took off at 12.40 hrs. Heading to the north-west, they took only 15 minutes to seek their prey. Thirty minutes later, having assembled into attack position, they closed in on a formation of B-17s, most probably from the 3rd Bombardment Division returning from bombing Rostock and Stettin. *Sturmstaffel* 1 shot down one B-17, whilst pilots of IV./JG 3 shot down another nine.

The Eighth Air Force recorded what happened to the 3rd Bombardment Division: '*Immediately after the bombing assault, 30 to 35 Fw 190s and Me 109s began aggressive and vicious frontal attacks with enemy aircraft coming in abreast and flying through formations. At least 15 aircraft were lost in the combination of these attacks.*'

The Eighth Air Force reported 12 B-24s and 33 B-17s lost, including 11 that landed in neutral Sweden due to battle damage: I. *Jagdkorps* reported the loss of 36 aircraft with 13 German pilots reported killed, 17 wounded and a further 24 missing.

On 13 April 1944, aircraft manufacturing facilities and associated industries were again the targets for the Eighth Air Force as the American offensive switched to southern Germany. This time it was to be the turn of the ball-bearing factories at Schweinfurt, the Messerschmitt production plant at Augsburg, the Dornier plant at Oberpfaffenhofen and Lechfeld airfield. Five hundred and sixty six of the 626 bombers despatched were effective over their assigned targets escorted by nearly 900 fighters. *Sturmstaffel* 1 and IV./JG 3 took-off following an *Alarmstart* at 12.45 hrs, forming up into a *Geschwader*-based *Gefechtsverband* with the *Stab*, I. and II./JG 3. Towards 14.00 hrs, enemy condensation trails were sighted east of Giessen at 6,500 metres, but the formation was flying with an immensely strong escort of P-51 Mustangs. At 14.00 hrs over Aschaffenburg, the German formation launched a frontal attack against the third wave of bombers. Ignoring the Mustangs and powering through a formation of some 150 B-17s, the Fw 190s of *Sturmstaffel* 1 shot down five *Viermots* in a matter of seconds.

The Eighth Air Force recorded: '*Of the three Bombardment Divisions,*[the] *1st met the heaviest air opposition... Around 14.00, another series of attacks was launched 10 minutes before Schweinfurt and continued for about half an hour. The lead Combat Wing, which sustained the heaviest losses was first attacked at about 13.50 near Klingenberg. Eight B-17s of the high group were shot down in about three minutes...*'

The onslaught against the German aircraft industry continued with the Eighth Air Force mounting attacks on a range of targets around Berlin including Oranienburg, Perleberg, Brandenburg and Rathenow on 18 April.

The tactical partnership of *Sturmstaffel* 1 and IV./JG 3 was ordered into the air at 13.30 hrs, but bad weather prevented assembly with other units and it was only these two units, together with Bf 109s of the *Wilde Sau* unit II./JG 302 from Ludwigslust, which carried out a close-formation attack on some 350 B-17s escorted by 100 fighters. Sixty kilometres west of Berlin, *Sturmstaffel* 1 attacked first, with *Gefr*. Wolfgang Kosse claiming one of the Fortresses as his 21st victory and *Uffz*. Kurt Röhrich another, as his eighth. From 6./JG 302, *Ofw*. Eberhard Kroker claimed a *Herausschuss* over a B-17, his second victory in two days, though the *Gruppe* would unfortunately suffer the loss of the *Staffelkapitän* of its 4. *Staffel*, *Oblt*. Willi Klein, when he was shot down over Alberode near Eschwege.

Closely following the *Sturmstaffel*, IV./JG 3 again showed its mettle by claiming no fewer than 19 B-17s destroyed, though the actual American losses for the entire mission were 19 B-17s including one aircraft which was interned in Sweden. Only one pilot was lost from IV./JG 3. This not insignificant accomplishment was deemed sufficient to gain *Major* Friedrich-Karl Müller a mention in the official *Wehrmacht* bulletin of the day.

Following the events of 29 April 1944, when Berlin was again the target, a German press reporter wrote: '*When, at noon on Saturday, the sirens wailed over Berlin and, a little later, single groups of US gangster aircraft appeared over the capital to drop their terror bombs aimlessly on a wide-spread residential area of the city, the operation rooms of the German air defences had been working at a high pitch for a long time...*'

The Eighth Air Force committed 368 B-17s and 210 B-24s for this attack on the German capital, while another 38 B-17s were to attack various targets of opportunity in the Berlin and Magdeburg areas. Escort was to be provided by 814 USAAF fighters.

To meet the Americans, I. *Jagdkorps* was ready to deploy 275 single- and twin-engined fighters. According to the *Korp's* war diary: '*From 07.25 hours, the German intercept service was able to locate the assembly of 11 combat wings. Commencing at 09.15 hrs, 600 bombers, 400 single-engine and 200 twin-engine fighters took off from the Great Yarmouth area to fly an offensive mission in an easterly direction towards Berlin. They crossed the Zuider Zee, towards Hannover and Soltau and struck at Berlin flying by way of Stendal and Pritzwalk.*'

At 10.10 hrs, *Sturmstaffel* 1 and IV./JG 3 took off together from Salzwedel led by *Lt*. Hans Weik, *Staffelkapitän* of 10./JG 3. Once assembled with other *Gruppen* from the *Reichsverteidigung* over Magdeburg, at 10.45 hrs, the *Gefechtsverband* headed towards Braunschweig. Shortly before 11.00 hrs, the German formation sighted the American bombers and Weik turned his aircraft 180 degrees to launch a frontal attack.

LEFT: FhjObfw. Willi Unger of 11.(Sturm)/JG 3 in the cockpit of an Fw 190 A-8 at Salzwedel. Although already an accomplished glider pilot when he joined the Luftwaffe at the beginning of the war, Unger served first as an aircraft mechanic and was not accepted for pilot training until December 1941. Eventually joining 11./JG 3 in March 1944, his first confirmed victory was a B-17 which he shot down on 11 April, and by the end of that month he had nine victories, two of which were Herausschüsse. When IV./JG 3 became a Sturmgruppe at the end of April, Unger flew with 12.(Sturm)/JG 3 and in August he was promoted to Oberfeldwebel. He was recommended for the Ritterkreuz after 19 victories, although by the time it was awarded on 23 October, Unger had raised his score to 21 victories, all of them four-engined bombers. After being commissioned as a Leutnant and attending a formation leaders' course, he became Staffelführer of 14.(Sturm)/JG 3 which, together with the rest of IV.(Sturm)/JG 3, had moved to the Eastern Front in February 1945. Leading the 14. Staffel on freie Jagd and ground-attack missions, Lt. Unger claimed a P-39 on 19 February and two Pe-2s on 15 March, bringing his tally to 24 victories. At the beginning of April 1945, Unger joined JG 7 but, although he successfully converted to the Me 262, he achieved no more victories and at the end of the war became a PoW of the Americans.

Simultaneously, and in conformity with its tactical doctrine, the *Sturmstaffel* formed up for a rearward attack on another part of the formation, trusting in its armour-plated cockpits to afford the pilots protection whilst closing in to killing range.

By the time the *Gefechstverband* had finished its work, nine B-17s had gone down under the guns of IV./JG 3 including two claims from Weik and one each from *Uffz*. Walter Loos and *Uffz*. Willi Unger, both of 11./JG 3. All three of these pilots would be awarded the *Ritterkreuz* later in the war. For its part, the *Sturmstaffel* had accounted for a further 13 Fortresses.

The Eighth Air Force reported: '*The 4A Combat Wing experienced difficulty with PFF equipment and lost visual contact with other bombers and fighter escort. Reaching the Magdeburg area, the Wing was attacked by packs estimated as totalling 100 enemy aircraft which attacked in waves from nose to tail. Attacks were pressed home vigorously and closely and lasted for about 20 minutes. The Wing lost a total of 18 B-17s.*'

Altogether, the Berlin raid cost the Americans 38 B-17s and 25 B-24s with a total of 18 crewmen killed and 606 missing. The war diary of I. *Jagdkorps* recorded: '*In spite of good visibility and high numerical strength, the large-scale attack on Berlin was, for the American air force, no success of great importance in respect to the overall war effort. Industry in Berlin sustained only slight damage. Damage to buildings and the losses of personnel were heavy. The strafing attacks on airfields showed no results...*'

The German press was quick to exploit what had been perceived as a failure for the Eighth Air Force and a victory for the *Luftwaffe*: '*One of the biggest air battles ever fought!*' proclaimed a *Luftwaffe* reporter. '*US fighters inferior to Messerschmitts and Focke-Wulfs... The fierce onslaught by German fighters increased in violence when the enemy bombers reached the Berlin area... Any order among the bomber formations was visibly shaken from the moment the big air battle over the Elbe began...*'

Meanwhile, on 15 April *Generalleutnant* Galland had visited Salzwedel to brief officers of the *Geschwaderstab* JG 3 and Stab IV./JG 3. Accompanying him was *Hptm*. Wilhelm Moritz, whom the *General der Jagdflieger* introduced as the new *Gruppenkommandeur* of IV. *Gruppe*, replacing *Hptm*. Heinz Lang who had stepped briefly into the role following *Major* Friedrich-Karl Müller's appointment as *Geschwaderkommodore*. Moritz was an experienced fighter pilot who had joined JG 3 from 11./JG 51 in October 1943.

During the meeting, Galland spoke of his plans for the tactical reorganisation of IV./JG 3. During the 'Big Week' raids of early 1944, pilots such as Hans Weik, Willi Unger and Hans Iffland had achieved impressive personal victories against the *Viermots*. Indeed, as a result of the whole *Gruppe's* encouragingly consistent successes against the bombers, Galland intended to convert the unit into a fully-fledged *Sturmgruppe* which would opperate in accordance with the tactical doctrine of the original *Sturmstaffel* but in *Gruppe* strength. Galland also intended that every *Geschwader* operating in the defence of the *Reich* would eventually include its own *Sturmgruppe*. Reaction to this proposal on the part of IV./JG 3's pilots however, appears to have been mixed and led to considerable debate. Though Galland's reasoning was appreciated, many officers felt that it was unnecessary to sign oaths and documents of obligation in the same way as the *Sturmstaffel*, let alone volunteer for tactics which would involve ramming or court-martial, when those already employed were achieving results.

Moritz recalled: "*When I took over the leadership of the Sturmstaffel at Salzwedel, the two ranking officers of the unit, von Kornatzki and Bacsila, were not fit for action; one was ill, the other wounded. I have to admit that my relationship with these two officers was not the best because I had the impression that they allowed their Staffel to go into action without their leadership. This was not acceptable practice for responsible officers. In their absence, Lt. Gerth led the Staffel on operations. For my part, I never accepted the fighting tactic favoured by von Kornatzki and never bound a pilot to ram a bomber. My IV./JG 3 scored many victories attacking bombers with traditional tactics and their successes rested on the sense of duty and the tactics of my men, namely attacking in closed formation and opening fire at close quarters.*"

Perhaps the most immediate change for the *Gruppe* however, was Galland's plan to replace its Bf 109 G-6s with the more heavily armed and armoured Fw 190 A-8, an aircraft considered better suited to the role of close-range *Sturmjäger*. The Fw 190 A-8/R2 – many of which would equip the *Sturmgruppen* – featured two 20 mm MG 151 cannon installed in the wingroots and two 30 mm MK 108 cannon in the wings. The cowl-mounted MG 131 machine guns fitted to the standard A-8 were removed to reduce weight and the gun troughs were covered with armoured plate. Additionally, a panel of 6 mm armoured glass was mounted on each side of the cockpit canopy and a sheet of 6 mm armour plate, extending from the lower edge of the cockpit canopy to the wing root, was mounted externally on each side of the fuselage to protect the pilot from lateral fire. Another armoured panel on the underside of the aircraft protected the pilot's seat to a point sufficiently forward to protect his feet and legs.

Fw. Willi Unger of 11.(*Sturm*)/JG 3 summarised the Fw 190 A-8 thus: "*Advantages: wide undercarriage, large twin-row radial engine which protected the pilot from fire from the front, electric starter motor and electric trim system. Disadvantages: there was a danger of turning over when braking hard on soft or sandy ground. In combat against enemy fighters, more awkward because of the heavy armour plating. Strong at low altitudes, inferior to the Me 109 at higher altitudes. In my opinion, the Fw 190 – in this version – was the best aircraft used in formation against the Viermots.*"

On 29 April, the day the Eighth Air Force bombed Berlin, an order was received from OKL officially redesignating IV./JG 3, under the command of *Hptm*. Moritz, to IV.(*Sturm*)/JG 3 in line with Galland's intentions. *Sturmstaffel* 1 was dissolved and its pilots and ground crews formed the nucleus of 11.(*Sturm*)/JG 3 under the command of *Lt*. Werner Gerth.

On 8 May, the targets were again Berlin and Braunschweig. Nearly 750 B-17s and B-24s escorted by more than 729 fighters reached Germany, with the B-24s of the 2nd Bombardment Division leading the formation in a straight line to Berlin, passing over the Zuider Zee and onwards, north of Hannover. East of Uelzen, the 2nd Bombardment Division, together with the 45th Combat Wing from the 3rd Bombardment Division which had become separated from the Berlin force, turned south to bomb Braunschweig.

ABOVE: FhjObfw. Willi Unger. This photograph was taken in the autumn of 1944 when Unger flew with 11.(Sturm)/JG 3. Note the 'Whites of the Eyes' emblem painted above the left breast pocket of his flight jacket.

At 08.42 hrs, IV.(*Sturm*)/JG 3 together with *Stab*/JG 3 were airborne to intercept. At 10.00 hrs, despite worsening weather, contact was made with the B-24s. *Fw*. Oskar Bösch remembers events clearly:

"*I particularly remember the 8 May mission, the details of which are engraved in my memory and which went wrong from the beginning. We were flying at 3,000 metres beside a box of B-24s at a slightly lower altitude when our own Flak mistook us for a target! A shell exploded near my aircraft and riddled it with shrapnel. Almost immediately, a trail of oil appeared on my windscreen and canopy. An oil pipe had been hit. I called on the radio to my comrades that I had to leave the flight. This I did without losing a minute; getting closer and closer to the B-24s. As I flew down through the bomber formation, I found that I had to fire at the last B-24 which burst into fragments. I continued to fire as I flew through the formation but I had no time to observe the results because, in a brief matter of time, I had passed through some 60-plus bombers.*

"*I was in a relatively secure position – in between the bombers where I could not be fired at without the gunners risking hitting one of their own bombers. Out of ammunition and over-excited, I decided to ram one! I moved into an oblique attack on a B-24. I could feel the buffeting from the slipstream. My aircraft was thrown off-balance and I missed my intended victim by only a few metres. Then the sky became clear in front of me. Looking around, I could see no bombers, only some kind of hell of fire. My plane vibrated as shots hit home and I am sure that the lateral armour plating saved my life. Pushing my stick forward, regardless of the terrific negative G forces, I was now in a straight dive, (at 1,000 km/h), engulfed in bullets and hits. Without wasting time, I undid my harness and jettisoned the canopy; a freezing wind snatched me from my seat. I felt terrified during my free-fall of 6,000 metres as I waited to pass through the clouds before opening my parachute. I landed at Goslar in the Harz. I was lucky to have been only lightly wounded in the head by some shrapnel and slightly burned on the face from my fall in the freezing air, because my parachute had been pierced many times by bullets!*"

USAAF Intelligence later reported: '*The B-24s attacking Brunswick were strongly attacked in the target area... Some mass attacks were made, but the majority of passes were made by groups of four to eight, head-on, level, and slightly high out of the sun...The formation was subjected to fierce fighter opposition in the Nienburg area when nearing Brunswick without escort. About 75 enemy aircraft, mostly*

Fw 190s, attacked in a square block formation, massing and assaulting from the nose. These pilots were experienced and viciously aggressive, pressing so closely that in one instance a bomber was destroyed by collision with an enemy fighter...'

Oskar Bösch was credited with a B-24 *Herausschuss* following this operation while IV.(*Sturm*)/JG 3's total claims amounted to 19 *Abschüsse* and *Herausschüsse*, compared with the loss of 11 B-24s plus a further seven subsequently written off.

Since March 1944, General Carl Spaatz, commander of USSTAF, had been closely monitoring Germany's oil storage and production capacity. The bombing policy directive issued by Sir Arthur Tedder on 17 April 1944 to Sir Arthur Harris and Spaatz stipulated that: '*... the overall mission of the strategical Air Forces remains the progressive destruction and dislocation of the German military, industrial and economic system, and the destruction of vital elements of lines of communications. In the execution of this overall mission the immediate objective is first the destruction of German combat strength, by the successful prosecution of the combined bomber offensive.*'

Despite the omission of oil as a specific target, two days after the directive, Eisenhower provided Spaatz with verbal authority to proceed with a "limited offensive" against German oil targets. Encouraged, Spaatz ordered the Eighth Air Force's commander, General Doolittle, to begin attacking as many oil targets in central Germany as possible. However, the weather gave the Germans a badly needed respite and it was not until 12 May that the first massed bomber formations, drawn from 15 combat wings with an escort provided by the USAAF and the RAF, headed out on a carefully-plotted course to bomb the synthetic production plants at Zwickau, Merseburg-Leuna, Brüx and Lützkendorf. Once again, however, the skilful German fighter controllers had been watching developments and in a refreshingly successful operation sent up to intercept them a total force of 470 single- and twin-engined fighters from JG 1, JG 3, JG 5, JG 11, JG 26, JG 27, JG 53 and ZG 26. These harassed the bombers from Frankfurt to the targets in well co-ordinated attacks and the Americans reported confronting the largest numbers of *Zerstörer* for several weeks. Some even reported rammings and the sheer aggression of the attacks forced at least one combat wing to become completely disorganised and lose contact with half its bombers. By the end of the day, the strike force had lost 46 bombers. For the *Luftwaffe* however, the cost had again been high, with losses in the I. *Jagdkorps* sector amounting to 34 aircraft destroyed with a further 31 written off due to damage in excess of 60 per cent.

On the 28th, a record 1,341 heavies were dispatched against six oil and rail targets in Germany, but nearly 500 were forced to abort due to the weather. Against the balance of this force, I. *Jagdkorps* deployed 333 single- and twin-engined fighters, of which 266 engaged in combat. The bombers caused heavy damage to a tank depot at Magdeburg, a sugar refinery at Dessau and three hydrogenation plants.

Among the units sent to intercept the bombers aiming for Magdeburg was *Hptm.* Ernst Düllberg's III./JG 27 whose Bf 109 G-6s took off from Götzendorf/Leitha at 12.47 hrs. Over the Wittenberg area of central Germany however, the *Gruppe* sighted a small formation of B-17s on its way to bomb the Junkers works at Dessau and engaged the *Viermots* at some 7,000 metres over the small town of Zerbst to the east of Magdeburg. Flying as a *Kettenführer* with 8./JG 27 was *Uffz.* Hans-Joachim Burkel who selected a B-17 and made his approach from behind, below and to the right of the bomber and opened fire with his MG 151/20 cannon at 350 metres range. Closing to 200 metres, he saw hits in both starboard engines and the Fortress started to burn and trail dense smoke. Burkel then saw crew members bale out, but was not able to see the bomber go down as a pair of P-51 escort fighters appeared and unsuccessfully attempted to attack him. Burkel was able to escape and land safely at Bürnburg, following which he was awarded a *Herausschuss* – his second – along with four other pilots from the *Gruppe*. III./JG 27 also claimed eight B-17s shot down for the loss of Günther Weth of 7./JG 27. Three other aircraft were also lost but the pilots survived.

The I. *Jagdkorps* recorded a total 39 aircraft destroyed, five missing and 34 badly damaged. The Americans lost 26 B-17s and six B-24s as well as 14 escort fighters.

Major Anton Hackl, *Gruppenkommandeur* of III./JG 11, an *Eichenlaubeträger* with more than 150 victories to his credit, was one of the *Luftwaffe's* principal tacticians and a leading 'bomber killer'. On 20 May 1944, he sent a paper to Galland in which he offered his suggestions on what was required to deal with the *Viermots*:

'*The aim of all fighter formations in operation against bombers when the target of the bomber stream is known, should be:*

a) To attack as late as possible, causing bombers to jettison even though a late approach excludes the possibility of a second operation, or –

b) To attack as early as possible, thus allowing Gruppe after Gruppe to attack at minute intervals. Allied fighter relief would then be forced to deal with the main body of attacking elements, one after the other, necessitating a splitting of forces and would not be in a position to hamper individual Gruppen making repeated frontal attacks, even where there was Allied high-altitude fighter cover. Secondly, on the second sortie, auxiliary tanks should be retained as far as possible in order to challenge Allied formations as deep as possible inside the Reich. Fighter protection is less bold and weaker here, and relief does not always arrive as scheduled. Thirdly, it is certainly possible to break up Allied formations through these tactics; rear attacks are then possible so that even bad gunners would have to get a victory or be suspected of cowardice. Experience of frontal attacks shows that only older [experienced] pilots get victories and for the most part, they get hit. Younger pilots do not approach correctly, nor go in near enough. Fourthly, my Gruppe proposes therefore 1) to bring over continually from the Russian Front young pilots with few victories so that the East would become a kind of battle school for the West and 2) every pilot, even when his ammunition has been expended, must attack in formation as long as the Kommandeur does, in order to split up defence and prevent our own pilots refusing combat.'

The same day that Hackl drafted his paper, Galland summoned *Major* Walter Dahl, the commander of III./JG 3, to a meeting at Wiesbaden-Erbenheim. Galland advised Dahl that he had been monitoring the operations of his *Gruppe* – one of the most successful units serving in the *Reichsverteidigung* – for the past few months and congratulated him on his considerable achievements. Since the first daylight raid on Berlin in March 1944, there had been pressure on the command of the *Jagdwaffe* to improve the control and co-ordination of the fragmented *Gruppen* based in the *Reich* in order to launch quick, concentrated responses to the American bomber threat. The *General der Jagdflieger* had put forward proposals for the formation of a special *Gefechtsverband* in *Geschwaderstab* strength known as the *Jagdgeschwader zur besonderen Verwendung (JGzbV)*. This would oversee a number of *Jagdgruppen* based in southern Germany under 7. *Jagddivision* and which would operate as a cohesive force with the prime role of attacking bombers from both the US Eighth and Fifteenth Air Forces. It was hoped lessons would be learned and experience gained. On 23 April 1944, *Major* Gerhard Michalski, the *Kommandeur* of II./JG 53 and a veteran *Jagdflieger* of the Mediterranean Front who wore the *Ritterkreuz*, was appointed to set up the *Stab JGzbV* at Kassel. On 1 May however, just days after his appointment, Michalski was wounded in action and was temporarily assigned as a unit leader instructor. Galland subsequently asked Dahl if he would lead the *JGzbV*.

Dahl agreed enthusiastically and after further discussions with *Major* Gerd Müller-Trimbusch, Galland's Chief-of-Staff, flew back to his unit the same day to put things into immediate effect, firstly overseeing the transfer of the *Gruppe* from Bad-Wörishofen to Ansbach. The next day, 21 May, Dahl – still at Wörishofen – officially handed over command of III./JG 3 to *Hptm.* Karl-Heinz Langer, formerly the *Staffelkapitän* of 7./JG 3. He then left for Ansbach where he had established the headquarters of the new *Jagdgeschwader zbV*. In the meantime Müller-Trimbusch had assigned five *Jagdgruppen* to Dahl: III./JG 3 under Langer at Ansbach; I./JG 5 under *Major* Horst Carganico at Herzognaurach (planned as high-altitude escort fighters with the Bf 109 G-6/AS); II./JG 27 under *Hptm.* Ludwig Franzisket at Unterschlauersbach; II./JG 53 under *Hptm.* Julius Meimburg at Frankfurt-Eschborn; and III./JG 54 under *Hptm.* Werner Schroer at Lüneberg.

On 24 May, the *JGzbV* flew its first major operation against the enemy in which a successful engagement was made against some of the 517 B-17s which set out to bomb Berlin under cover of nearly 400 escort fighters. The I. *Jagdkorps* threw 255 single-engined fighters against the raid, drawn from the 1., 2., 3., and 7. *Jagddivision*. Bounced by P-51s over Rangsdorf, the German force, believed to have comprised elements of

ABOVE: An obviously posed photograph of ground crews of III./JG 11 watching a victory bar being applied to the rudder of Major Anton Hackl's Fw 190 A-6. This represented Major Hackl's 141st victory, a B-24 which he shot down on 11 April 1944. Note that, as the Kommandeur of II./JG 11, the entire tail of Hackl's aircraft has been painted white to identify the formation leader. During an attack against bomber formations, individual aircraft of a unit often became separated and the white rudder assisted pilots in reforming.

II./JG 27, II./JG 53 and III./JG 54, engaged in a massive, violent fighter-versus-fighter air battle in which only a few aircraft succeeded in breaking through to the bombers. The Fw 190s of III./JG 54 accounted for ten B-17s (including three *Herausschüsse*). Thirty-three B-17s were lost and a further 256 damaged. An ebullient Dahl sent a glowing report of events to Galland.

Three days later, on 27 May, the US 3rd Bombardment Division despatched 102 B-17s to bomb aircraft industry targets and a marshalling yard at Strasbourg in France and a further 98 Fortresses to strike a railway yard in Karlsruhe. The *JGzbV* ordered I./JG 5 airborne at 11.00 hrs to intercept the bombers heading for Strasbourg, and the *Gruppe* clashed with enemy fighters over the Alcase, losing seven pilots including – as has been related earlier – *Major* Carganico, the *Gruppenkommandeur*.

At 11.30 hrs III./JG 3 took off with 21 Bf 109s and headed for Karlsruhe. *Ofw.* Georg Ströbele claimed a B-17 destroyed and *Hptm.* Langer, a *Herausschuss*. Operating together, II./JG 27 and II./JG 53 engaged B-17s in the vicinity of Nancy at 12.15 hrs. The former *Gruppe* managed to destroy two Mustangs and a B-17, while II./JG 53's *Ofw.* Herbert Rollwage claimed one of the unit's score of three B-17s, plus a P-51. However II./JG 27 lost three pilots and six Bf 109s to enemy action, including *Fw.* Rudolf Philipp of 6. *Staffel*, one of the unit's most accomplished pilots, and II./JG 53 reported the loss of one pilot killed and another wounded.

The fact was that throughout May, I. *Jagdkorps* still found it increasingly difficult to concentrate its forces against large-scale American raids as its units were scattered across the Reich, had to fly great distances to reach the bombers and required long periods to assemble into *Gefechtvervbände*. Consequently, German fighters were often late in intercepting the *Viermots* or were forced to land early as a result of fuel shortage. *Fw.* Willi Unger of 11./JG 3 recalled: "*The operational bases of our fighter units in the Reichsverteidigung were spread all over Germany. Attempts to maintain strength at critical times and in critical areas were made by the rapid redeployment of fighters to northern or southern Germany. Several Gruppen from various airfields would combine in the air and were then led from the ground to attack the approaching bombers. This did not always work. The bombers often cheated by flying towards one town before changing course to bomb a completely different target. As the endurance of our fighters flying with an auxiliary drop tank was a maximum 2.5 hours, we were often forced to break off. There is no question of German fighters having the advantage, only disadvantages, since the numbers of American escort fighters were far superior to us and they also operated at higher altitude.*"

On 29 May, in response to a raid by the US Fifteenth Air Force against the Messerschmitt works at Wiener-Neustadt, a lack of radio communication within a *Gefechtsverband* comprising IV.(*Sturm*)/JG 3 and elements from JG 300 which had just started large-scale daylight fighter operations, led to confusion and the break up of the formation. Amidst the confusion, the aircraft flown by *Major* Friedrich-Karl Müller, the *Kommodore* of JG 3 collided with another machine and was forced to crash-land at Salzwedel. Müller was killed in the crash and having flown some 600 missions, his death added to the growing list of valued formation leaders who had been killed defending the German homeland.

Schmid summarised the month of May 1944 thus: "*American fighters, the strength of which had increased considerably, were in a position to demonstrate their air superiority in various respects. Especially impressive was the perfect and accurate cover they provided for the bombers as they made their incursions and also as they returned to their bases. The fighter escort, flying up to an hour ahead of the bombers, made the commitment of German air defence against the bombers extremely difficult and sometimes even impossible. Whenever German fighter units did succeed in attacking an American bomber stream, American fighters arrived on the scene in a surprisinngly short time.*"

I. *Jagdkorps* calculated that the ratio of total American air superiority (bombers and fighters) to German strength was 7.7 to 1, while in fighters alone, the ratio was 3.8 to 1 in favour of the Americans.

Meanwhile, the OKL had been encouraged by the performance of the *Sturmstaffel* and with IV.(*Sturm*)/JG 3. It was decided to increase the strength of the *Sturmgruppe* in late May by assigning to it 2./JG 51, an Fw 190-equipped *Staffel* which had returned from the Eastern Front under the command of the very experienced *Oblt.* Horst Haase. Haase's *Staffel* would eventually be fully integrated into IV.(*Sturm*)/JG 3 as 16. *Staffel* in August. Furthermore, OKL ordered the establishment of two new *Sturmgruppen*, II.(*Sturm*)/JG 4 and II.(*Sturm*)/JG 300.

In mid-May 1944, *Obstlt.* von Kornatzki was ordered to set up II.(*Sturm*)/JG 4 at Salzwedel and Welzow. As the new *Gruppe's* air and ground personnel had previously served with 1./ZG 1, which had been equipped with Ju 88s and employed against Allied convoys in the Atlantic, Kornatzki decided that to assist him he would gather together a solid core of pilots from *Sturmstaffel* 1 who understood what was required of them and possessed the necessary combat experience. Consequently, a number pilots from *Sturmstaffel 1* – including *Fw.* Gerhard Marburg, who became Kornazki's wingman – joined the *Gruppe*, and the former Ju 88 pilots were hastily converted to the Fw 190 at Hohensalza.

The first of the *Gruppe's* own Fw 190 A-8/R2s, however, did not arrive until late July, and for most of the summer its personnel underwent further conversion and technical and tactical training. Nevertheless, by the end of July, the composition of the new *Sturmgruppe* was as follows:

Stab, II.(*Sturm*)/JG 4	*Obstlt.* Hans-Günter von Kornatzki (newly promoted)
5.(*Sturm*)/JG 4	*Hptm.* Wilhelm Fulda (replaced soon after by *Hptm.* Erich Jugel)
6.(*Sturm*)/JG 4	*Hptm.* Manfred Köpcke
7.(*Sturm*)/JG 4	*Oblt.* Othmar Zehart

However, the *Gruppe* had to wait until late July to receive its first Fw 190 A-8/R2s and for most of the summer its personnel underwent conversion, technical and tactical training.

LEFT AND OPPOSITE TOP AND CENTRE: In May 1944, during a short stay at Barth, a Schwarm of Fw 190s from 12./JG 3 took part in trials during which a single, rearward-firing 21 cm mortar tube was fitted beneath the aircraft's centre section. The idea was that the pilot would fire the mortar after he had made a firing pass against a bomber formation and had passed through the bomber box. The installation was known as the 'Krebsgerät', or 'Crab Device', but it proved mechanically unreliable and generally unsatisfactory. The additional armour added to the Fw 190 had already affected its performance and Uffz. Willi Unger, one of the pilots who took part in the trials and who is shown here with his 'Yellow 17', stated that the weight of the weapon caused a further deterioration in the aircraft's speed and manoeuvrability. Other reports mention the weapon's inherent inaccuracy and the consequent risk to other attacking German aircraft. The strake on the mortar tube was part of a device which retained the mortar shell within the tube.

Focke-Wulf Fw 190 A-8/R2 'Yellow 17' flown by Uffz. Willi Unger of 12./JG 3, Barth, May 1944
This profile shows Uffz. Unger's 'Yellow 17' fitted with extra cockpit armour and equipped with a WGr.21 'Krebsgerät' below the fuselage. The aircraft is finished in a standard 74/75/76 scheme and has a white band around the rear fuselage upon which is superimposed the black wavy bar of IV. Gruppe. Note the MG 151/20 and MK 108 armament in the wings and that the fuselage MG 131 machine guns have been removed and the blast troughs faired over.

BELOW: A line-up of Fw 190s from IV.(Sturm)/JG 3, all of which are armed with a single, rearward-firing WGr. 21 mortar tube.

Geschwader Identification Bands

One of the difficulties encountered by German pilots operating against US bomber formations was that they became scattered after each attack and valuable time was wasted in reforming on formation leaders for a repeat attack. Therefore, in order to make the aircraft flown by the Staffelkapitän or Gruppenkommandeur more easily recognisable from a distance, the rudders or whole vertical tail surfaces on their machines were painted white. This arrangement seems to have worked well enough until larger numbers of fighters from several units were employed simultaneously, and to meet this eventuality, in the spring of 1943, JG 1 began painting black and white stripes on the engine cowlings of its Fw 190s and in the summer, parts of JG 1 began painting the engine cowlings of their aircraft with a black and white chequered pattern.

At the same time, as the requirement arose for additional units to distinguish their aircraft from those of others, some home defence units began painting coloured bands around the rear fuselages of their machines. One of the first units to adopt the coloured fuselage band was JG 11 which, in mid-1943, used a narrow white band. The aircraft of JG 1 flew with a red fuselage band in addition to their striped or chequered cowlings, and in the autumn, the dedicated anti-bomber unit Sturmstaffel 1 began using a wide black/white/black band narrowly edged each side in white. At about the same time, JG 11 seems to have changed its bands to yellow, possibly because their thin white band was too easily confused at any distance with the white in the bands used by Sturmstaffel 1. The use of this system was obviously effective because, also in the autumn of 1943, JG 1 dispensed with the cowling markings in favour of a wide red band around the rear fuselage. By early 1944, the

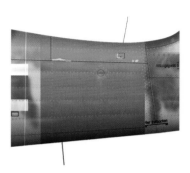

JG 1

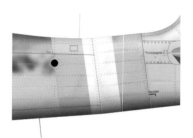

JG 2

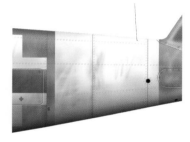

JG 3

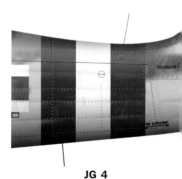

JG 4

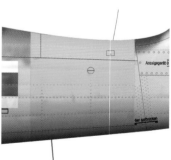

JG 11

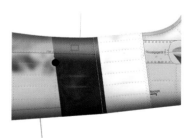

JG 26

JG 27

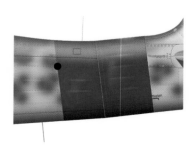

JG 54

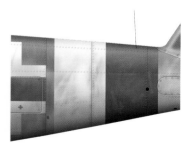

JG 77

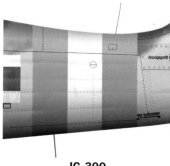

JG 300

aircraft of those parts of JG 27 engaged in home defence had bright green fuselage bands while some Gruppen of JG 3 had white bands.

Unfortunately, no original German documentation concerning the unit identification bands seems to exist, and the earliest official reference to them is found in an Allied intercept of a signal transmitted on behalf of Reichmarschall Göring and dated 24 December 1944. The Allied translation of this states that, 'Jagdgeschwader will be marked with 90 cm coloured band round fuselage for better differentiation. Each Geschwader to have different colours or combination of colours.'

Today, these bands are usually, but erroneously, referred to as Reichsverteidigung, or Defence of the Reich bands, but it is interesting to reflect that Reichsverteidigung was not a word mentioned in either this or a later order which, moreover, clearly state that their purpose was unit identification.

Also interesting is the fact that the bands had been in use for some considerable time before the December order. Equally curious is that a further two months would elapse before the issue of any confirmation concerning the precise colours, or combination of colours, to be used by each Jagdgeschwader. Again, the only reference to this order, B.Br.Nr2/25 g.Kdos dated 20 February 1945, is an Allied translation which states:

'By order of the Reichsmarschall and for purposes of improving aerial recognition, Jagdgeschwader aircraft are to be marked by fuselage-encircling coloured stripes as indicated in the appended enclosure. Attention of troops down to platoon level is to be drawn to these markings which should simplify the recognition and distinction of our own aircraft.'

The translation then goes on to detail the colours and colour combinations to be used by each unit, although the tone of the colours actually used sometimes differed from what was specified. The greatest variation concerns the reference to the use of a bright blue, as specified for JG 54 and JG 300, whereas the tone actually used was sometimes a dark blue. It should also be noted that some units, especially those operating in the East, had no need of these bands, and while JG 51, for example, may, therefore, not have used the bands at all, other units later omitted to apply them to new or replacement aircraft. In this respect, while JG 4 is known to have employed its prescribed white/black/white bands at the end of 1944, new Fw 190 D-9s delivered in 1945 often did not. It is therefore true to say that, paradoxically, by the time the Luftwaffe issued the official order confirming which colours were to be employed, they were already falling into disuse.

No official documentation, German or Allied, has been discovered detailing the checked bands known to have been used by the Kampfgeschwader (J), the former bomber units operating in the fighter role. Some of these units were equipped with the Me 262 but the only two Geschwader to apply checked bands were KG(J) 6 and KG(J) 54. The colour combinations used by these units have now become known as a result of post-war research and have therefore been included in the following colour illustrations.

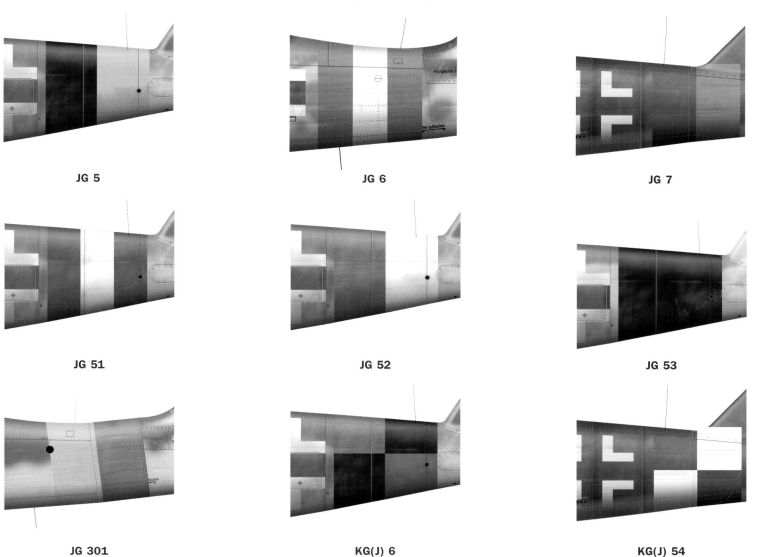

JG 5   JG 6   JG 7

JG 51   JG 52   JG 53

JG 301   KG(J) 6   KG(J) 54

Invasion

With the economic and military infrastructure of the *Reich* directly threatened by the burgeoning Allied air offensive, accusations began to mount that the German fighter force was inadequate and incapable. Describing the condition of the *Jagdwaffe* a few days before the Invasion, Schmid wrote: '*Heavy losses as well as the great physical and psychological strain imposed on German fighter pilots reduced the combat value of our units in April and May 1944. The young replacements showed deficiencies in flying and radio usage. They lacked combat experience, particularly in respect to high-altitude operations. Time and opportunities for training in the operational units was lacking to an increasing extent. The shortage of qualified formation leaders increased. The excessive strain caused by almost uninterrupted commitment resulted in combat fatigue. Experienced fighter pilots reached the limit of their efficiency. They were worn out by the many missions they had flown and needed a rest. All these factors resulted in a number of failed missions.*

'*For the first time, branches of the Wehrmacht, Luftwaffe, Government and Party unjustifiably reproached the fighter units of the home air defence for cowardice. In view of these accusations, it should be noted that the inferior German day fighter forces fought bravely and were subjected – especially in May – to the heaviest strain, which admittedly reduced the substance of their personnel and materiel, yet did not seriously obstruct the overall structure of these forces. The limited American offensive activities against the Reich's territory in the first week of June offered the day fighter forces of the home air defence a brief respite for regeneration. Thus, it was possible that the day fighter Geschwader were reasonably intact and ready for defensive operations against the Invasion in France.*

ABOVE: Generalleutnant Josef Schmid (second from right) the commander of I. Jagdkorps from mid-September 1943 to the end of November 1944, discussing the measures to be implemented in the event of an Allied landing. On the far left is Oberst Walter Oesau, a Schwertenträger and Kommodore of JG 1 who was shot down and killed on 11 May 1944. Unfortunately, the identity of the two officers standing with Oesau is not known although both are wearing the Ritterkreuz.

LEFT: The Geschwaderkommodore of JG 26, Obstlt. Josef Priller, at Guyancourt, the base of II./JG 26, soon after the Allied landings had taken place. Obstlt. Priller and his wingman, Ogfr. Heinz Wodarcyk, flew the only true German fighters to make an appearance over the Allied beachhead on the morning of D-Day when they made a single strafing pass over British troops on 'Sword' beach shortly after 08.00 hrs. The very first Luftwaffe daylight sorties flown in the invasion area by a day combat unit, however, are attributable to some Fw 190 fighter-bombers of 3./SKG 10 from Rosières which claimed four Lancaster bombers over the Cotentin peninsula between 05.01 and 05.04 hrs.

On 6 June, the Allies landed in France, pouring 155,000 men and their vehicles and equipment onto the Normandy beaches on this day alone. The Allied air cover was immense, with sufficient capability to fly more than 14,500 sorties within the first 24 hours. Only two *Luftwaffe* fighter sorties were flown that morning when the *Geschwaderkommodore* of JG 26, *Obstlt.* Josef Priller and his wingman swooped in at 15 metres over the British landing area at 'Sword' beach, their Fw 190s raking disembarking troops and armour with cannon and machine gun fire.

ABOVE: Ground personnel pushing Obstlt. Priller's 'Black 13' under cover in June 1944. Priller led the Geschwader from 11 January 1943 until 27 January 1945 when, already having been promoted to Oberst on 1 January, he left to take up the position of Inspector of Day Fighters (West). In a combat career lasting five years on the Western Front, Priller flew his final operational sortie during Operation Bodenplatte on 1 January. With a final tally of 101 victories, he was decorated with the Swords and survived the war. Post-war, he took over the family's brewery business and died of a heart attack in 1961.

In the early hours, the OKL teleprinters clattered out the string of warnings and situation reports from the respective *Jagdkorps* headquarters, but the vital instruction to proceed with the transfer of the home defence units to the invasion zone never materialised. OKL dithered in indecision. The threat of bad weather over the central German mountain range risked jeopardising the whole transfer and late that morning, despite misgivings voiced by Galland, I. *Jagdkorps* acted unilaterally and ordered the transfer to proceed. By early afternoon the first units began to move, though the bad weather prevented many from transferring until evening, and by the morning of the 7th, 400 fighters had arrived in France. June 6th had seen II. *Jagdkorps* operate a total of only 121 aircraft. When contacted, Göring was bewildered at OKL's lack of reaction.

Within days however, just under 1,000 fighters drawn from JG 1, JG 3, JG 11, JG 27, JG 77 and JG 301 had arrived from Germany. These aircraft moved into a 100 km-long belt of airfields constructed by *Luftflotte 3* running parallel to the Channel coast – but then the debacle began. *Oberst* von Lachemair recorded: '*The transfer operation was, as everything was at that time, only a drop in the bucket, merely the action of a poor man. This drop was unable to bring about any change in the overall situation.*'

The Chief-of-Staff of II. *Jagdkorps* reported: '*Our own day fighter forces were at first employed exclusively on low-level attacks on landing craft and landing points and as fighter cover for the fighter-bomber formations of Fliegerkorps II which were attacking the same objectives. Often the enemy's superior fighter defence intercepted our own formations before they could reach the Invasion Front and after the latter had run out of ammunition and fuel they were forced to return without having carried out their actual mission.*'

Operating from barely prepared emergency strips – most of them without sufficient buildings, ammunition or fuel facilities and completely lacking dispersal points, blast shelters, teleprinter and radio installations, the German fighters struggled throughout June and July to make even a dent in the overwhelming Allied strength. As early as mid-June, *Luftflotte* 3 had lost 75 per cent of the strength it possessed immediately prior to the landings and units were plagued with technical problems and accidents. The Allied air forces constantly strafed and bombed the airfields and a new pilot, lacking in training and flying time, was lucky to survive more than three sorties. *Major* Hans-Ekkehard Bob commanded II./JG 3 operating out of Dreux; he recalled: "*We were often attacked taking off, causing one aircraft taking off to be blocked by another. Our position was extremely unpleasant. We reckoned in operating strength we were outnumbered ten to one. In fact, operations were really more an exercise in self-preservation.*"

Self-preservation must have been uppermost in the minds of the men of II./JG 1 in the days immediately following the Invasion when the unit was based at Le Mans and under the temporary command of *Oblt.* Rüdiger Kirchmayr. On the night of 9/10 June, 109 RAF Lancasters and Halifaxes led by Pathfinder Mosquitoes bombed the airfield. Many of the *Gruppe's* Fw 190s and vehicles were destroyed or damaged and the unit was subsequently grounded while the 300 bomb craters which scarred the airfield's surface were filled in and numerous unexploded bombs rendered safe. Finally, after days of frustrating inactivity, the unit moved to Essay, which was also bombed three days later, forcing another transfer to Semalle, a rough landing strip some six kilometres north-east of Alencon. By late July, although II./JG 1 was able to report a relatively full complement of pilots, most of these were new arrivals from the training schools and none of the *Gruppe's* component *Staffeln* possessed an experienced *Staffelkapitän*. Instead, they relied on temporary, field-appointed *Staffelführer*, two of whom were experienced NCOs.

Ofw. Herbert Kaiser, an experienced NCO, was one of the pilots rushed to Normandy in June 1944. Despite being considered a combat veteran by his fellow pilots, Kaiser remembered the air fighting on the Invasion Front as being some of the toughest; he recalled the *Luftwaffe* being "*... ground into the earth*" and that:

"*At the end of June 1944, I was with 7./JG 1 on an airfield just outside Paris and experienced an excellent example of the almost complete Allied air superiority. We were detailed to intercept a formation of incoming Allied bombers in the Normandy area. We had to take off in the smallest of flights (usually two to four aircraft)* due to the Allied fighters which almost always waited above our airfields for our fighters to emerge from cloud cover. We would be forced to sneak towards the target area by hedge-hopping over the terrain to take advantage of as much natural camouflage as possible. Flying just a few metres above the ground kept us off the radar screens, but sometimes put us into the side of a hill. We would only climb to altitude once we reached the point of attack.*

"My flight of four aircraft sighted a formation of escorting Spitfires and we positioned ourselves to engage them. But right at that moment, we were jumped by another formation of Allied fighters and in the process I lost all three of my fellow pilots. Escape for me seemed impossible and it was only because of my experience as a flier that I was able to get myself into some nearby cloud and save my skin.

"At this time the odds were against us and you could count on the fingers of one hand the days you expected to live. Frankly, I am amazed Luftwaffe fighter pilots had any nerve left at all, let alone the ability to attempt to fight under such conditions."

ABOVE: This Fw 190 A-8, 'Black 5', in Normandy is believed to be the aircraft flown by Obgfr. Max-Ulrich Förster of 2./JG 1 who was posted missing after being shot down by US fighters on 28 July 1944.

On 9 August, Kaiser's *Staffel* was assigned to intercept a formation of some 300 Allied aircraft. Preparing to attack a group of RAF Lancasters, he was bounced from the sun by Spitfires near Paris and his Bf 109 G received severe damage. Badly wounded, Kaiser jettisoned the canopy of his burning fighter and baled out, but his right leg became entangled in his parachute lines. He landed behind German lines with multiple fractures to his right thigh and was hospitalised in Germany until February 1945.

After spending several days with units in the West Galland wrote:

'*My impressions were shattering. In addition to the appalling conditions, there was a far-reaching decline in morale. This feeling of irrevocable inferiority, the heavy losses, the hopelessness of the fighting, which had never before been so clearly demonstrated to us, the reproaches from above, the disrepute into which the Luftwaffe had fallen among the other arms of the forces from no fault of the individual, together with all the other burdens that the war at this stage had brought to every German, were the most severe test ever experienced by the Luftwaffe.*'

The 4. and 5. *Jagddivisionen* had concentrated the four *Jagdgeschwader* under their command in the Paris-Lille area, but it soon became evident that even Lille was over exposed to danger. German fighters were forced to take off as soon as plots of enemy aircraft were received, if they were not to run the risk of being pinned to the ground by prowling enemy fighters and, even with drop tanks, this often resulted in German fighters being short of fuel by the time they were expected to engage US bombers. Consequently, II. *Jagdkorps* suggested the withdrawal of these fighters into the Reims-Romilly-Creil area – but as a result of poor preparation and the risk of

LEFT: After seeing action with III./JG 77 over Poland, the Channel, the Balkans, Russia, North Africa and Italy, for which he was awarded the Ritterkreuz in March 1943 after 53 victories, FhjOfw. Herbert Kaiser joined JG 1 in March 1944. On 9 August, his aircraft was one of a formation that took off to intercept a daylight raid by Lancaster bombers, during which sortie he was shot down by escort fighters. Kaiser baled out of his Bf 109 G-6 'White 12' but was seriously injured when he struck the fin and did not return to operations until February 1945. He then joined JV 44 and survived the war with 68 victories.

overcrowding on these more easterly airfields, which were already being used by *Luftwaffe* bomber and night fighter units – this did not take place.

The operations of a *Jagdgruppe* over the Invasion Front in June 1944 is typified by the experiences of *Hptm.* Karl-Heinz Langer's III./JG 3. On 6 June, this *Gruppe* transferred its 45 Bf 109s together with an advance detachment of ground crew and equipment in eight Ju 52s from Ansbach to St. André-de-l'Eure, a reasonably-equipped airfield with concrete runways, south of Évreux. The rest of the *Gruppe's* personnel and equipment followed by road.

Operating under the command of *Generalleutnant* Bülowius' II. *Fliegerkorps*, the unit went straight into action the following day, when 28 of its Messerschmitts attacked shipping and landing craft at the mouth of the Orne. Later in the day, the *Gruppe* sent up 18 Bf 109s to escort fighter-bombers attacking enemy armour. Six pilots were shot down or lost to shipborne Flak and 75 per cent of the aircraft which saw operations were

ABOVE: German prisoners of war and armour and artillery of the British Second Army in Normandy in early August 1944. Allied strategy in Normandy called for British and Canadian armies to draw the attention of the best of the German armoured forces, including the elite Panzer Lehr and Waffen-SS divisions, onto their front while the Americans, on the right flank, broke out to the west in a roundabout route towards Paris. This eventually proved successful, but German resistance throughout the Normandy campaign was tenacious and the original Allied objectives were only achieved after many weeks of heavy fighting. Possibly the most contentious phase of the campaign began shortly after this photograph was taken with the battle for Falaise and the attempt to close the Falaise pocket. Note the short lengths of track welded to the front of the tanks as increased protection against armour-piercing shot.

reported damaged to some degree. Over the next three days, III./JG 3 bombed shipping targets with 250 kg bombs, engaged P-47s and P-51s and acted as escort for fighter-bombers and bombers over the Orne. On the 9th, the RAF bombed St. André and the *Gruppe* was forced to transfer to Marcilly, a poorly-equipped airfield five kilometres to the south. This inconvenience was countered to some extent the following day when the unit claimed three Mustangs shot down.

Following a day when the unit flew three fighter-bomber missions against landing craft, another transfer ensued on the 13th when the *Gruppe* moved to Francheville from where it operated under 5. *Jagddivision*. Over the next two weeks, working with II./JG 3 and elements of JG 11, II./JG 53, JG 1, JG 26, JG 27 and III./JG 54, the unit flew several *freie Jagd* patrols plus fighter-bomber, ground-attack and tactical reconnaissance missions and engaged heavy bombers. Between 14-21 June, *Hptm.* Karl-Heinz Langer claimed a P-51 and a P-47; *Fw.* Paul Wielebinski, two P-51s; *Ofw.* Georg Ströbele, a P-51; *Fw.* Norbert Geyer, a P-38 and *Uffz.* Georg Küpp, a P-38. However, the unit suffered the loss of two pilots, including *Hptm.* Ulrich Bentsch and another pilot posted missing. Seven aircraft were damaged and two pilots were forced to bale out, including *Ofw.* Ströbele who was heavily wounded.

The following week, the *Gruppe* claimed another three Mustangs shot down, as well as a B-17, a B-24 and a Spitfire. The *Heer* also sent in a request that the unit conduct further ground-attack sorties during which four more pilots were lost and another five were posted missing. After being captured when his Bf 109 G-6 was shot down by enemy anti-aircraft fire near Bretteville-sur-Odon on 11 July 1944, *Lt.* Dieter Zink, the *Staffelführer* of 9./JG 3, told a fellow prisoner that:

"*Allied numerical superiority is quite colossal... You could say that their superiority in numbers is in the ratio of 20 to one, and then their materiel is better, and also their personnel. All our pilots are inexperienced, while theirs are all fairly experienced. Better aircraft, too – but there's nothing we can do about that. We had to stand on our airfield looking up at the sky, watching them fly over. We had six aircraft on the ground ready for operations and they used to circle about up there with between 80 and 100 aircraft. To take off is suicidal.*"

Perhaps the most drastic transfer was the movement of approximately 50 of IV./JG 3's Fw 190 A-8 *Sturmböcke* to the invasion zone, thus – briefly – depriving the defence of the *Reich* of its first, dedicated *Sturm* unit. The *Sturmjäger* arrived at Dreux from Salzwedel on the afternoon of 8 June with the first ground equipment and crews arriving in six Ju 52s shortly thereafter, but attempts at operations were continually disrupted by air raids and the threat of Allied fighters. It has been argued that the transfer of such heavily-armed and armoured fighters for work over Normandy was inappropriate but, equally, the Fw 190 A-8/R2s of 10. and 11./JG 3 perhaps offered greater protection to their pilots while deployed as *Jabos* and operating against shipping, landing craft and on battlefield support north of Caen, than did the Bf 109s and Fw 190s of other units (12./JG 3 was to act as escort to the other *Sturmstaffeln*). No casualties or aircraft losses were suffered by the unit while it was in Normandy, but on 10 June, Dreux was bombed by B-24 Liberators, and with the unit having achieved only marginal results it was decided to send it back to the *Reich*. By 15 June it was based at Eisenstadt, an airfield 45 km south-east of Vienna.

In committing virtually its entire defence force into the wasting cauldron of Normandy, the *Luftwaffe* made it easier for the Allies to resume their relentless strategic bombing campaign against the shrinking Reich and, in particular, against oil targets. During June, in the course of 17 major raids, 20,000 tons of bombs rained down on key oil installations in Germany, Hungary, Rumania and Bulgaria. Aviation fuel output had fallen from 214,000 tons in March to 120,000 tons in May and to 74,000 tons in June. At the beginning of June, *Luftwaffe* fuel stocks stood at 540,000 tons but by 1 July, this was down to 218,400 tons.

On the 17th, Stumpff ordered the units under his command at *Luftflotte Reich* to actively conserve fuel: '*The fuel situation and the present rate of consumption at the front necessitate the imposition of immediate measures to save fuel. Only by making utmost reductions, above all in general air activity and also in operations, will it be possible to overcome the present situation. Unnecessary use of fuel is equivalent to sabotaging the war effort.*'

The Operations Staff at *Luftflotte Reich* also evaluated the operations in June in a report to OKL. It made sombre reading: '*As a result of the Invasion, the main effort of fighter commitment was, to a considerable extent, shifted to the area of Luftflotte 3. The relief of Reich territory from enemy air attack which had been expected as a result of the Invasion, was realised to only a very small extent. On the contrary, the enemy directed the main effort of his offensive action against those war production plants most important at the time, against fighter production and, above all, against oil supply. Further effective support on all defensive fronts, especially the West, can be insured only if there is an undisturbed production of aircraft and the required fuel. Only then can an acceptable balance of power in the air be maintained.*'

The report continued: '*It is therefore of decisive importance for the outcome of the war, that primarily petrol supply does not suffer any further interruption. The systematic and continued attacks against oil production constitute, at present, the most acute danger.*'

Meanwhile, as a result of the transfer of fighter units to France, the defence of the *Reich* was now left seriously depleted. Immediately after the Invasion, only a scratch force was left to intercept US daylight raids. This comprised the single-engined *Wilde Sau* night fighter *Gruppen*, four twin-engine *Zerstörer Gruppen*, three *Ergänzungsjagdgruppen* in Silesia and East Prussia, some fighter school units, a Bf 109-equipped Hungarian fighter unit and *Erprobungskommando* 16, the test unit equipped with a small number of rocket-powered Me 163s.

Strangled by the rapid advance of the Soviet Army in the East and the Allies in the West and to the South, the *Reich* found itself starved of fuel, threatened on every front and facing round-the-clock bombardment.

On 20 June 1944, *Oberst* Ulrich Diesing, a former *Zerstörer* pilot attached to the staff of the *Chef der Technischen Luftrüstung* at the RLM, addressed a gathering of *Gauleiter* and local officials as the representative of the *Generalluftzeugmeister*, *Generalfeldmarschall* Erhard Milch:

BELOW: An unusual view of Fw 190 A-8 'Black 10', the aircraft flown by Hptm. Robert Weiss, Kommandeur of III./JG 54, at Villacoublay in June 1944. Just visible on the rear fuselage is the wide blue band allocated to JG 54 when flying in the Defence of the Reich, upon which is a superimposed III. Gruppe bar. In September 1944, III./JG 54 became the first operational Luftwaffe unit to receive the new Fw 190 D-9.

'In regard to day fighters, our defences have already shown an improvement. But operations are still shouting for more and more aircraft, and with justification – for we have to combat not only enemy fighters but also hordes of four-engined bombers, which constitute a formidable adversary, particularly during the day.

'We must therefore far exceed our present production. The opportunity is there... All our fighters are capable of being used offensively and of carrying bombs. That was done because in addition to the grave threat of the four-engined bomber to our homeland, the danger of invasion was obvious. We are all aware that the fate of the war rests with the Invasion. The Invasion has now been with us for fourteen days. Now the enemy has a foothold on the Continent. But there is no cause for alarm. We must master the situation, and from what we hear it can be mastered, provided that we rapidly build up a front-line air force on a par with the enemy.

'Yesterday, I spoke with General Galland, who had come back from the front. Galland stated quite clearly that as far as performance goes, our fighters are adequate and indeed in most cases superior at the altitudes at which the Invasion fighting is taking place, but that unfortunately, they were by no means sufficient in numbers. The morale of our fighter pilots, however, was high, as high as in the days of the great offensives on the Western and Eastern Fronts. A considerable number of enemy aircraft have been shot down. To name but one example, in the initial stages, Oberstleutnant [Josef] Priller [Kommodore, JG 26], had five successive kills... The problem now is to provide the necessary numbers. If we can keep up a supply of these aircraft to the front during the next few months, I believe that we shall be able to force a decision in the air war. I believe that a decision must come this summer... Our aircrews have the spirit to fly these fighters and they have the faith that they can turn the tide of battle against our enemies in the West, however bitter the struggle.'

THIS PAGE: Ground personnel carrying out last minute checks on a well-concealed Bf 109 G in the summer of 1944. The cut branches which were placed over the front of the aircraft have been moved aside (*LEFT*) and in the photograph (*BELOW RIGHT*), taken shortly before the pilot started the engine, a mechanic may be seen assisting with the straps.

ABOVE AND RIGHT: A similar scene to that on the previous page with ground personnel working on an Fw 190 A-8, W.Nr. 690140.

LEFT: Ground crew removing the covers from an already bombed-up Bf 109 G-6 fighter-bomber of the Gruppenstab of II./JG 3 at Evreux shortly after the Allied landings in Normandy. The spinner has a white spiral and the winged 'U' badge of JG 3 'Udet' has been applied to the engine cowling. Around the rear fuselage is the white unit identification band assigned to JG 3, upon which is the horizontal bar of II. Gruppe in black. The markings ahead of the fuselage Balkenkreuz are thought to comprise a black chevron and the number '1', both edged in white, which may indicate that the aircraft was flown by Oblt. Max-Bruno Fischer, the Gruppen Adjutant.

BELOW: A Bf 109 G-6 of JG 3 in the summer of 1944. Although perhaps also taken at Evreux at the same time and location as the photograph above, this may not be the same machine.

THIS PAGE: The decision to deploy the heavily armed and armoured fighters of IV./JG 3 to attack ground and waterborne targets in Normandy with SC 250 bombs seems to have been justified by the fact that the armour offered such protection that no pilot casualties or aircraft losses were incurred. In this sequence of photographs, 'Black 8', an Fw 190 A-8/R2 flown by Uffz. Willi Maximowitz of 11./JG 3, is seen returning to Dreux after a sortie over the invasion beaches.

Focke-Wulf Fw 190 A-8/R2 'Black 8' flown by Uffz. Willi Maximowitz of 11./JG 3, June 1944
Although camouflaged in a perfectly standard scheme of 74/75/76, the finish on this machine was considerably enhanced by the decorative black cowling and the stylised eagle's wings on the fuselage sides. Superimposed on the engine cowling was the winged 'U' of JG 3, the 'Udet' Geschwader, and the IV. Gruppe bar appeared on this Geschwader's white rear fuselage band. Although incongruous, the yellow spiral on the spinner and the red outline to the fuselage are believed to be correct.

LEFT AND BELOW: An Fw 190 A-8 which was left behind in France by retreating German forces in 1944. The aircraft had the tactical number 'Yellow 1' and was finished in the standard 74/75/76 day fighter scheme of the time. This aircraft was produced at the Focke-Wulf factory at Cottbus in July or August 1944 and lacks the yellow panel under the nose which had been employed as a recognition aid for several years. On 25 June 1944, a somewhat ambiguous order had been issued stating that, with immediate effect, all Luftflotte 3 aircraft were to be marked only with a spiral on the spinner and that with the exception of the Balkenkreuz, tactical numbers and Gruppe bars, all other markings were to be removed. However, given the unclear wording of the original signal, while the intention may have been to ensure that any spinner design other than the spiral was forbidden, it may equally have applied to the yellow panel under the nose and any unit badges.

BELOW AND BELOW RIGHT: Another Fw 190 found by Allied forces in France was this Fw 190 F-8, W.Nr. 581443 photographed at Brétigny with damage suggesting that a demolition charge had been placed near the engine before the machine was abandoned. Standard day fighter camouflage had been applied and although the aircraft carried no operational markings, the front of the engine cowling had been painted yellow.

ABOVE AND RIGHT: The appearance of this Bf 109 G found at Rheims is typical of the finish applied to Bf 109s in 1944, although in this instance the machine has no operational markings. The camouflage scheme consists of the colours 74, 75 and 76 with regular, round mottles on the fuselage sides and, also typical of the period, is the grey centre to the fuselage cross which contrasts with the black of the swastika on the fin. Less typical, however, is the spinner, which has the appearance of being white with a black spiral, instead of the opposite way around.

Mass against Mass 2 – *Sturmgruppen*

While the bulk of the German daylight fighter force in the West was fighting its battles over France, there was still the need to provide an adequate and effective air defence over the *Reich*. In accordance with the Allies' strategic plan, the scale of damage inflicted as a result of their bombing offensive was beginning to take a serious effect on German production capability. In reporting to the *Jägerstab* on 30 June 1944, *Generalstabs.-Ing.* Roluf Lucht described what he had seen during a recent tour of aircraft production plants in the Leipzig and Magdeburg areas: *"From above, Oschersleben looked devastated. All the sticks of bombs missed the target, but incendiaries fell right on the works. There were major fires. They will probably be able to carry on production except for small parts, where it is too early to tell. They have lost ten to twelve aircraft. Four Mustangs were shot down and destroyed when they hit the ground. The factory gun detachment did its best to defend; the works representative was firing too. They brought down one of the raiders but that was all... At Bernburg – little damage. Two aircraft hit, one hangar wrecked. There was nothing in it – just a small fighter hangar. A second assembly shop received four direct hits, but it will be fully working again today. For the present they are working under the open sky..."*

BELOW: An Fw 190 A-8, its propeller wash raising the dust, taxiing from its dispersal.

BELOW: Seen here as a Leutnant, Hans Weik, the Staffelkapitän of 10.(Sturm)/JG 3, was credited with the destruction of 22 four-engined bombers. He was awarded the Ritterkreuz on 27 July 1944 and ended the war with the rank of Hauptmann.

Seven days later, the aircraft and synthetic oil plants were targeted again by the Eighth Air Force when it sent 939 B-17s and B-24s escorted by more than 650 fighters to attack a range of targets in central Germany, but this time the defenders were ready and they were to inflict a devastating blow on the Americans. As the B-24 Liberators of the 492nd BG approached Oschersleben from the west, a *Gefechtsverband* led by the recently appointed *Kommodore* of JG 300, *Major* Walther Dahl, and comprising the 44 Fw 190 A-8s of *Hptm*. Wilhelm Moritz' IV.(*Sturm*)/JG 3 from Illesheim, escorted by Bf 109 G-10s from I., II., and III./JG 300, evaded the fighter escort and closed in on the Bomb Group's Low Squadron. It had been planned initially to make a frontal attack against the bombers, but this was changed to a rear attack, made at 09.40 hrs, 5,600 metres over Oschersleben. Despite the massed defensive fire from the bombers, the Fw 190s spread across the sky line abreast, in a formidable broad front and closed to 100 metres before opening fire. It took the *Sturmböcke* about a minute to shoot down 11 Liberators – an entire squadron, and when the B-24s of the 2nd Air Division returned home, 28 of their number had been lost, most of them to the *Sturmgruppe* which had lost nine of its own aircraft in the attack. Altogether, the Eighth Air Force lost 37 heavy bombers with another 390 damaged during the day's raid. Wilhelm Moritz claimed a *Herausschuss* for his 40th victory, while *Lt.* Hans Weik, *Staffelkapitän* of 10.(*Sturm*)/JG 3, who would receive the *Ritterkreuz* on 20 July, claimed a B-24 for his 35th. Other notable claims were lodged by pilots who had become leading masters in the art of destroying bombers; *Fw.* Hans Schäfer of 10.(*Sturm*)/JG 3 who shot down two Liberators in five minutes for his 16th and 17th victories; *Fw.* Willi Unger of 12.(*Sturm*)/JG 3, his 10th and 11th, and *Lt.* Werner Gerth of 11.(*Sturm*)/JG 3, his 13th and 14th. In one of their earliest missions as day fighters, the pilots of JG 300 also claimed nearly 30 aircraft shot down or shot out of formation.

ABOVE: Major Walther Dahl, Kommodore of JG 300, examining his specially decorated Fw 190 A-8 'Blue 13', W.Nr. 170994, at Finsterwalde after his 75th victory in July 1944.

Such decisive success was attributable to the determined mass against mass tactics employed by the *Sturmgruppen* during the summer and autumn of 1944. Typically, if, in the opinion of senior German fighter controllers, prevailing clear weather indicated the possibility of an incoming daylight raid as well as large-scale defensive operations, the regional *Jagddivision* would telephone either the *Gefechtsverbandführer* or the *Kommodore* of a *Jagdgeschwader* which operated a *Sturmgruppe*. Once German radar and listening services had detected enemy formations or radio traffic, the entire *Sturmgruppe* would be brought to 15 minutes readiness and the formation leader would then relay this information to his *Gruppenkommandeure*. They in turn would then hold a pre-briefing with their pilots. The *Geschwader* HQ – which would usually have been in operation since dawn – would assign a 'Y'-aircraft for fighter control purposes, as well as issue call signs and advise the chain of command.

Once confirmation of an incoming raid had been received from the Division – usually at the point when enemy bombers were either assembling or crossing the English coast – the *Geschwader* would go onto three minutes readiness. As more information arrived, the pilots would be moved forward to *Sitzbereitschaft*, or cockpit readiness, and appraised of further developments via loudspeaker at the dispersal point.

At the order to scramble, all three *Gruppen* would then take off and, within six to ten minutes, assemble over their own airfields at 900-1,800 metres before flying to the *Gefechtsverband* assembly point where, under strict radio discipline and control, the *Gefechtsverbandführer* formed up the whole battle formation. The formation assembly usually took place at 3,000 metres and had to be complete within about 20 minutes. The formation would then climb to a combat altitude of 7,500 - 8,000 metres.

In the case of IV.(*Sturm*)/JG 3, following assembly, the *Gruppe's* Fw 190s flew in two stacked down *Sturmkeil* or Vee formations each comprising eight to ten aircraft from the *Stab* and three *Staffeln* (depending on serviceability), the second formation flying 140-180 metres behind and about 45 metres below the lead formation. Meanwhile, the Bf 109 *Begleitgruppen* (escorts) would split to either side of the *Sturmgruppe*, stacked up from front to rear. Another, smaller escort – usually formed from the aircraft of 2./JG 51, later 16./JG 3 – would fly high cover at about 900 metres above the rearmost aircraft of the second Vee of the *Sturmgruppe*. The Bf 109s would fly in a sufficiently loose formation to avoid slipstream and allow aircraft to weave without the risk of collision.

Within sight of the enemy bomber formation and some 90-150 metres above and 900-1,520 metres behind it, the aircraft of the *Sturmgruppe* would release their external tanks, then reform from the Vee formation into an *Angriffsformation* (attack formation) or *Breitkeil*. This was carried out by spreading out into a slightly swept-back, line abreast formation of usually more than 20 fighters level with or slightly above the enemy, with the commander of the *Gruppe* and his deputy flying at the apex. As Walther Dahl explained to his Allied captors in September 1945: "*Upon sighting the enemy bomber formation, the formation leader gives the signal to attack by rocking his wings, or by radio. The wings of the Vics now pull up until the aircraft are in line abreast, with the formation leader throttling back a bit so the others can catch up. The approach is made from behind and the fighters attack in a line, the formation leader dividing up the target according to the formation of bombers, for example: Bomber formation on a broad front with little*

BELOW: Major Walther Dahl, Kommodore of JG 300 (centre) in discussion with Hptm. Wilhelm Moritz, Kommandeur of IV.(Sturm)/JG 3 (right) and Hptm. Heinz Lang of Stab IV.(Sturm)/JG 3 at Memmingen in late July 1944.

depth (from top to bottom). The CO will attack the centre, and the forces to right and left will go to right and left respectively.'"

In cases where the interval between the bomber formation selected for attack and the succeeding bomber group within the stream was reasonably large, the *Sturmböcke*, or 'Battering Rams', found little difficulty in manoeuvring into a favourable attacking position, but when bomber groups flew more closely together, it was necessary to make a very tight formation turn which demanded total concentration.

Once the Focke-Wulfs were in position, and upon clearance being received from the *Jagddivision*, the formation leader gave the order to attack over his FuG 16ZY radio, together with instructions for re-assembly afterwards. Each pilot selected one bomber as his target, closed in to about 360 metres and, aiming at the tail gunner, opened fire with his two 20 mm MG 151 wingroot cannon. As the *Angriffskeil* closed to 180 metres, each pilot opened fire with his 30 mm MK 108 cannon, now aiming at either of the inboard engines. Should the selected bomber have been damaged or set on fire by a fellow pilot, a *Sturmjäger* would move through the formation and pick another target. Having made their attack, some pilots broke away 45 metres from the bomber and sideslipped in the direction of the reassembly area on the basis that this was the quickest and safest means to get clear of defensive fire and debris. Others either broke away after passing their target bombers or passed further through the formation before slipping out. Dahl maintained that exit from a *Pulk* should be made "*... to the side and down and reassemble at the same altitude with the bombers about 3,000 yards to the side and 1,000 yards below. The basic principle to be observed in reassembling is that the assembly is to be made on the same side from which the entry into the bomber stream was made. The advantage thus gained is that the escort Gruppen are on the right side after the attack to protect the reassembly of the Sturmgruppe without having to change sides. If little or no further opposition is encountered, a second attack can be carried out by the Sturmgruppe.*"

Variations to the basic tactics did occur; for example the pre-attack flight formation of II.(*Sturm*)/JG 4 usually consisted of three stacked down Vees, unlike IV.(*Sturm*)/JG 3's two-formation method. Furthermore, pilots of II.(*Sturm*)/JG 4 are reputed to have favoured diving below the level of the bomber formation prior to making an attack, nosing up immediately before opening fire.

On 18 July, more than 500 B-17s and B-24s of the US Fifteenth Air Force operating from Italian bases attempted to strike at the aircraft production facility at Manzell. At the same time, an attack was made against Memmingen airfield in southern Germany, to which IV.(*Sturm*)/JG 3 had recently moved, though it was the presence of 70 Bf 110 and Me 410 *Zerstörer* trainers there which had caught the attention of USAAF reconnaissance. A force of around 45 Fw 190s of IV.(*Sturm*)/JG 3 was scrambled to intercept the raid. Assembling over Holzkirchen, the *Gruppe* headed south towards the *Viermots* which were reported to be approaching from Innsbrück and Garmisch. For the second time in less than two weeks, the *Gruppe* hacked down an impressive number of bombers – this time B-17s from the 5th Bomb Wing heavily escorted by P-51s and P-38s. Adverse weather prevented the greater part of the Memmingen force from hitting the target, forcing two Groups and their escort to turn back and another to bomb an alternative target. However, the Fortresses of the 483rd BG became separated, failed to receive the recall message and pressed on alone without their P-38 escort. As the 483rd doggedly neared the Starnberger See at around 10.50 hrs, the *Sturmgruppe* struck and 14 of the Group's Fortresses went down. In total, the pilots of IV.(*Sturm*)/JG 3, operating with 2./JG 51, claimed 34 B-17s shot down and 13 *Herausschüsse*. Two P-51s were also claimed.

Lt. Oskar Romm, a *Ritterkreuzträger* who had recently replaced *Lt.* Hans Rachner as *Staffelkapitän* of 12.(*Sturm*)/JG 3, claimed two B-17s and a P-51 as his 78th-80th victories, while *Oblt* Horst Haase, flying with 2./JG 51 accounted for his 49th victory. The *Gruppenkommandeur*, Wilhelm Moritz, claimed his 41st, and for his unit's accomplishments on 18 July he was awarded the *Ritterkreuz*. Several former *Sturmstaffel* 1 pilots proved their mettle: *Uffz.* Oskar Bösch of 11.(*Sturm*)/JG 3, *Fw.* Willi Maximowitz of 11.(*Sturm*)/JG 3, *Lt.* Werner Gerth of 11.(*Sturm*)/JG 3, *Fw.* Kurt Röhrich of 12.(*Sturm*)/JG 3 and *Fw.* Gerhard Vivroux of 11.(*Sturm*)/JG 3 claiming a total of seven victories.

One negative aspect of the 18 July operation was that, having broken away from the main JG 3 attack formation to shoot down a B-17 as his 36th victory, the Staffelkapitän of 10.(*Sturm*)/JG 3, Oblt. Hans Weik, was hit by the bomber's defensive fire which damaged his Fw 190 A-8/R2 and badly wounded him in the shoulder and arm. The loss of Weik's contribution to the *Sturmgruppe's* operations was a difficult one to bear as he was regarded as a fearless pilot and an inspiration to others in the *Gruppe*. He had joined I./JG 3 in February 1943 and scored ten victories before being transferred as an instructor to *Jagdgruppe Ost*. Returning to III. and then IV./JG 3 in the autumn of 1943, he

LEFT: A Bf 109 G-6 with Erla-Haube and a tall tail unit, probably in the summer of 1944. This machine is thought to have belonged to JG 27 and has the wavy bar of IV. Gruppe on the rear fuselage. Beneath this, however, is what appears to be an earlier II. Gruppe horizontal bar upon which is painted the name 'Margot'. With the gradual disappearance of unit emblems, decorating aircraft with the names of girlfriends, fiancées or wives became an increasingly popular alternative.

subsequently shot down 21 four-engined bombers in 85 operational missions. Weik mostly flew the Bf 109 and had survived being shot down on several occasions in early 1944.

Despite heavy losses, IV.(*Sturm*)/JG 3 continued to battle against the bombers for the rest of July and at the end of the month moved to Schongau, near the Austrian border, to operate against the US Fifteenth Air Force flying out of Italy. On 3 August, Fifteenth AF sent its B-17 and B-24s to bomb aircraft and steel factories at Friedrichshafen and chemical plants and the marshalling yards at Immenstadt, but by this time the entire *Gruppe* had only 16 aircraft and could put up only four *Schwärme*. The *Schwarm* from 12.(*Sturm*)/JG 3 was led by *Fw.* Willi Unger with *Uffz.* Hermann Christ, *Uffz.* Hans-Joachim Scholz and *Uffz.* Heinz Zimkeit. When the *Gruppe* took off to intercept the bombers which had raided Friedrichshafen, the raiders were returning to Italy, and as Unger later recalled:

"*The attack took place at 11.30 hrs at an altitude of 6,500 metres over the Lechtaler Alps. We shot down six Liberators, but during our attack the American escorts rushed at us from behind. As a result we lost eight Fw 190s to escort fighters and defensive fire from the bombers. Six German pilots met their deaths, two were able to bale out and landed high up in the Alps. Of my flight – four aircraft – only one machine made it back home. Two comrades were killed* [Uffz. Scholz and Uffz. Zimkeit]. *I myself was hit in the engine by fire from a tail gun. My windscreen went black with oil and I couldn't see a thing. I was saved by my parachute and landed with a thump some 2,000 metres up in the mountains. Fragments of my machine still lie scattered today at another spot up in the mountains. Of the six dead fighter pilots, two are still recorded as missing. Sixty-seven people were killed by bombs in Friedrichshafen, among them 22 Flak gun helpers aged 17. I took part in greater air battles over Germany, but for me, this was the most dramatic.*"

During the attack, Unger shot down one Liberator as his 15th victory. Christ and Scholz also each shot down a bomber and in total, IV.(*Sturm*)/JG 3 accounted for 19 B-24s either shot down or classified as *Herausschüsse*, but suffered the loss of five pilots and one wounded. Unger walked 16 kilometres to the nearest village where he found a car and arrived back at Schongau at midnight.

In May 1944, a third *Sturmgruppe* had begun forming up when the 4. and 5. *Staffeln* of the single-seat *Wilde Sau* night fighter *Gruppe*, II./JG 300 under the former reconnaissance pilot *Major* Kurd Peters, commenced conversion to the day fighter role together with I. and III./JG 300, commanded respectively by the former bomber pilots *Ritterkreuzträger*, *Hptm.* Gerhard Stamp and *Major* Iro Ilk [1]. Based successively at Dortmund, Merzhausen, Frankfurt/Main and Unterschlauersbach, II./JG 300 took delivery of new Fieseler-built Fw 190 A-8/R2s, while I. and III. *Gruppen* retained their Bf 109s for the escort role. In late June 1944, *Major* Walther Dahl relinquished command of his *Jagdgeschwader zbV* and was appointed *Kommodore* of JG 300.

Within II./JG 300, Dahl was able to draw on a number of battle-hardened pilots such as *Lt.* Klaus Bretschneider, one of the most successful and fearless *Wilde Sau* night fighters who had been credited with 14 victories in only 20 night missions during the first four months of 1944. Bretschneider was made *Staffelkapitän* of 5./JG 300 on 19 July. In addition, with IV.(*Sturm*)/JG 3's departure to France

---

1. The 6./JG 300 was detached from JG 300 to remain on night fighter operations as 8./NJG 11.

in June, a number of officers from *Oblt.* Horst Haase's 2./JG 51, which had been seconded to the original *Sturmgruppe*, were now temporarily detached to II./JG 300 to assist with training on the new Fw 190 *Sturmböcke*, while *Lt.* Oskar Romm of 11.(*Sturm*)/JG 3 went to I./JG 300 for similar purposes.

The new *Sturmgruppe* was officially designated II.(*Sturm*)/JG 300 in July 1944 and by 4 August, *Major* Peters reported to Dahl that the conversion and training of the unit for its new role was complete. Ten days later, on the 15th, II.(*Sturm*)/JG 300 received its baptism of fire.

It was a perfect summer day with a cloudless blue sky and almost limitless visibility. The Eighth Air Force used the conditions to despatch a force of nearly 900 B-17s and B-24s to bomb a range of airfield targets across Germany, including 219 B-17s of the 1st Bomb Division which were targeting airfields around Wiesbaden, Frankfurt and Köln. Of the 426 fighters sent to escort the strike force, 112 were assigned to the 1st Bomb Division.

The German listening services first reported the build-up of enemy bombers around 07.45 hrs and relayed the information to the various *Jagddivisionen*. At Bad Wörishofen, Walther Dahl placed his 100 or so available fighters on readiness and drew up plans for a *Gefechtsverband* comprising the *Geschwaderstabsschwarm* and I./JG 300 at Bad Wörishofen, II.(*Sturm*)/JG 300 at Holzkirchen and IV.(*Sturm*)/JG 3 at Schongau.

Within two hours, Dahl was airborne in his Fw 190 A-8 'Blue 13' accompanied by the 30 Bf 109 G-10s and G-14s of *Major* Stamp's *Höhenbegleitgruppe*. The formation headed south to Augsburg where it made a text-book rendezvous with the Fw 190s of the two *Sturmgruppen* just after 10.00 hrs. Under radio silence at 7,000 metres and with Dahl at the head of a great wedge-shaped battle formation, the German fighters turned towards Frankfurt, some 260 km away, in accordance with directions received from the 7. *Jagddivision*. Thirty minutes later, the Division ordered a change in course to Trier on the Mosel, 150 km further west, and passed control of the formation to *Obstlt.* Fritz Trübenbach, the *Jafü Mittelrhein* at Darmstadt.

After one hour's flying time and in slowly deteriorating weather, the *Gefechtsverband* finally sighted three *Pulks* of 60-80 Flying Fortresses of the 1st Bomb Division just west of the Mosel river and Dahl reported the observation to the *Jafü*, who gave clearance to attack.

Just before 11.45 hrs, Dahl manoeuvred his *Angriffskeil* for a classic attack from the rear, with Moritz's IV.(*Sturm*)/JG 3 assigned to the *Pulk* flying to his left and *Lt.* Bretschneider's II.(*Sturm*)/JG 300 the one on the right (*Major* Peters had broken a leg baling out of his aircraft a few days earlier). Dahl and the *Stabsschwarm* would tackle the centre *Pulk*.

Dahl lined up on a Fortress flying to the left of his selected group and opened fire at 300 metres. As he closed in, still firing, he saw hits and pieces flying off the bomber's fuselage and wings. A few seconds later, the B-17 veered to the left, with flames and smoke from the left wing trailing over the fuselage. Three crewmen baled out. As Dahl passed through the formation, the bomber lost its wing then nosed downwards.

The 303rd Bomb Group had 39 B-17s flying to bomb Wiesbaden airfield that day as part of the 41st Combat Wing, 1st Bomb Division. The Group was returning from having bombed the airfield, but its fighter escort had left the bombers and was not in sight when some 25 Fw 190s from Dahl's *Gefechtsverband* attacked the Low Group comprising aircraft from the 358th and 427th Bomb Squadrons. Nine out of 13 aircraft were shot down. 2/Lt. R.W. Davis was piloting B-17 *Flying Bison* of the 427th BS in the No. 4 position of the high element. He recalled (in third person narrative) the *Sturmgruppen's* devastating attack:

"*Immediately after being warned by tail gunner Sgt. W.F. Foley, Lt. Davis began violent evasive action. Two Fw 190s engaged them, making one pass before disappearing. Flying Bison sustained numerous hits, causing Lt. Davis to lose altitude from 22,000 to 17,500 ft and become separated from the rest of the formation. Fighting to get the aircraft back on an even keel, Lt. Davis began to take stock of his aircraft and crew. The engineer, Sgt. R.D. Hughes, had been instantly killed by a 20 mm cannon shell while flying in the waist gunner position. Radio operator Sgt. E.R. Gorman was wounded in his right ankle and tail gunner Sgt. Foley in the leg and foot. The navigator, Lt. G.L. Lange and the bombardier, F/O. F.W. Bryan, were sent back to administer first aid. Aircraft damage was very severe. The amplifiers and turbos were shot out, rudder controls were useless, the fuselage looked like a sieve, and the No. 4 engine was not functioning properly. The No. 4 propeller then ran away and was feathered. Fortunately cockpit instruments were all restarted but the engine began spurting oil and dropping pressure. It was again feathered for the remainder of the mission. To maintain the 17,500 ft altitude, airspeed was dropped to 140 mph. The wounded were made as comfortable as possible. Friendly fighters were attracted by firing flares and provided escort for the return journey... but the aircraft was damaged to such an extent that no attempt was made at repairs."*

Meanwhile, Dahl ordered his formation to reform and make a second attack. Selecting a second *Viermot*, Dahl once again closed in from 200 metres to 80 metres, firing with machine guns and cannon. The port inboard engine started to burn and the Fortress began to drop away from formation. Dahl hurriedly counted five parachutes, just as the American P-51 fighter escort arrived, at which point, with fuel now low, the *Sturmjäger* disengaged and turned for freshly-bombed Wiesbaden-Erbenheim and Mainz-Finthen, the nearest airfields cleared for their arrival, leaving Stamp's Bf 109s to take on the Mustangs.

When Dahl landed at Wiesbaden, his Focke-Wulf was rated as 35 per cent damaged as a result of defensive fire from the bombers, but 16 heavy bombers had been lost by the Eighth Air Force. Among the scorers from IV.(*Sturm*)/JG 3 were *Oblt.* Horst Haase from 16. *Staffel* (formerly 2./JG 51) who claimed one B-17 as his 51st victory; *Lt.* Werner Gerth of 14.(*Sturm*)/JG 3, a B-17 as his 23rd victory; and *Uffz.*

ABOVE: Uffz. Oskar Bösch with his Fw 190 A-8/R2 'Black 14' at Schöngau in August 1944 after transferring to 14.(Sturm)/JG 3. By the end of the year Bösch had been credited with nine victories and by the end of the war he was credited with 18. Of these, eight were four-engined bombers and three were obtained over the Eastern Front in March and April 1945.

Klaus Neumann and *Fw.* Kurt Gren, both of 16.(*Sturm*)/JG 3, who each claimed a B-17 as his 19th victory. One pilot was shot down and wounded as he baled out and another pilot, *Uffz.* Hermann Christ of 15.(*Sturm*)/JG 3, was killed in action.

Just under one month later on 11 September, *Obstlt.* von Kornatzki's II.(*Sturm*)/JG 4 flew one of its most successful operations against the bombers since its formation in the summer. That day the Eighth Air Force launched 1,016 heavy bombers from all three of its Bomb Divisions, escorted by 411 fighters, against eight synthetic oil plants as well as marshalling yards and an ordnance depot in central Germany. The I. *Jagdkorps* challenged this massive armada by fielding fighters from I. and IV.(*Sturm*)/JG 3; *Stab*, I., II.(*Sturm*) and III./JG 300; II.(*Sturm*) and III./JG 4; *Jagdgruppe* 10; *Stab*/JG 11; II./JG 27; III./JG 53; I. and III./JG 76 and the point defence Me 163s of I./JG 400.

At 10.30 hrs, II.(*Sturm*)/JG 4, with III./JG 4 providing its escort, received the *Startbefehl* and more than 60 Fw 190s and Bf 109s took off from Welzow and Alteno to form part of a *Gefechtsverband* which would fall under the tactical control of *Major* Günther Specht and the *Geschwaderstab* of JG 11. Under accurate guidance from the ground, the two *Gruppen* of JG 4 were vectored towards Chemnitz and at 12.10 hrs the unit had its first sighting of the bombers, though by this time aircraft from IV.(*Sturm*)/JG 3, I./JG 76 and II.(*Sturm*) and III./JG 300 were already engaging the 1st Bomb Division and its escort. JG 4 would take on elements of the 3rd Bomb Division south-west of Chemnitz with *Stab*/JG 11 and III./JG 4 deploying against the Spitfire and Mustang escort. *Major* Specht shot down one of the P-51 escorts for his 31st victory, while III./JG 4's Bf 109s accounted for two P-51s and two Spitfires shot down.

BELOW: Fw 190s of IV./JG 3 ready to take off from Schöngau in August 1944.

ABOVE: This aircraft, an Fw 190 A-8/R2, W.Nr. 681382, has been fitted with additional cockpit and canopy armour and was flown by Hptm. Wilhelm Moritz, the Kommandeur of IV./JG 3, who is seated on the cockpit sill. Moritz led IV./JG 3 from April 1944, received the Ritterkreuz in July and was promoted to Major in October, but by November he was no longer in command. The reasons for this remain obscure. While some sources state that he had been dismissed because he refused an order from Göring to take off in bad weather, an alternative and more likely possibility is that he was suffering from complete exhaustion as a result of the particularly arduous nature of his Sturmgruppe's attacks, most of which he insisted on leading himself. In any event, he later became Kommandeur of IV./EJG 1 and at the end of the war had 44 victories and was Kommandeur of II./JG 4. Perhaps somewhat surprisingly, his W.Nr. 681382 also survived the war and is recorded as having been at Neubiberg as late as 1946.

ABOVE: When Major Hackl left III./JG 11 in the summer of 1944, he became Kommodore of JG 76, a unit formed in June 1944 by converting the former Zerstörergeschwader 76 to the fighter role. The unit only consisted of the I. and III. Gruppen and in the autumn of 1944, I. Gruppe was redesignated IV./JG 300 and III./JG 76 became IV./JG 53. Shown here as Kommodore of JG 76 with his Fw 190 A-8 W.Nr. 170935 in the background, Major Hackl is wearing the Swords which he was awarded in July 1944 after 150 victories. He subsequently led JG 300 and later returned to JG 11 as Kommodore. Hackl survived the war with 192 victories, 32 of which were four-engined bombers.

Minutes later, at about 12.10 hrs and while the Allied fighter escort was occupied, II.(*Sturm*)/JG 4 went to work on the bombers. Their attack, carried out at an altitude of 8,000-9,000 metres, was so effective that 15 pilots, including *Hptm.* Manfred Köpcke, *Staffelkapitän* of 6.(*Sturm*)/JG 4 and *Hptm.* Erich Jugel, *Kapitän* of 5.(*Sturm*)/JG 4, each later claimed a B-17 shot down or as a *Herrauschuss*. But the attack had not been with out cost; 5.*Staffel* lost three pilots, 6.*Staffel* suffered five pilots lost and 7.(*Sturm*)/JG 4 lost three, all some 20 km south of Chemnitz.

Soon afterwards, at 12.19 hrs, the Fw 190s of 8.(*Sturm*)/JG 4, which had formed a high rear escort element for the *Sturmgruppe* in case the *Begleitjäger* of III./JG 4 were unable to offer sufficient protection, also waded in from the rear of the *Pulk* at around 8,000 metres. However, due to intervention by American fighters, their formation was not as tight as it should have been. Nevertheless, eight claims were made by eight pilots including the *Staffelkapitän*, *Hptm.* Gerhard Schroeder. One pilot, *Lt.* Alfred Rausch, rammed a B-17 with his Fw 190 A-8/R2 'Blue 16' over Reitzenhain/Komotau and was killed in the process. Apart from *Fw.* Josef Tüssner who was wounded, Rausch represented 8.(*Sturm*)/JG 4's only casualty.

By the end of the action, II.(*Sturm*)/JG 4 had claimed 16 Fortresses shot down with another seven classified as *Herrausschüsse*, while III./JG 4 claimed nine B-17s

LEFT: Bf 109 G-14s and G-6s of III./JG 300 at Jüterbog in June 1944.

destroyed with three *Herrausschüsse*, plus the four escort fighters. However, these victories came at a heavy price with II. *Gruppe* reporting 12 pilots lost, together with nine from III. *Gruppe*. The cost in aircraft was high too; JG 4 estimated that as a result of this operation, between a third and a half of its machines needed repair. Twenty-three Fw 190s were classified as 60-100 per cent damaged, with 27 Bf 109s reported at the same level.

For the USAAF, the cost was equally high with 40 heavy bombers and 17 fighters lost during the raid. But the next day, 12 September, JG 4 was to receive a further blow when *Obstlt.* von Kornatzki, the popular tactician and father of the *Sturm* concept was killed after an engagement with American bombers. During the late morning, he shot down a B-17 at 8,000 metres some 30 km west of Magdeburg during another US attack on the oil plants, but his aircraft was damaged by the bombers' defensive fire. Pursued by an American escort fighter, von Kornatzki attempted to make an emergency landing, but his Fw 190 A-8 crashed into some power lines at Zilly near Halberstadt. *Major* Gerhard Schroeder, *Staffelkapitän* of 8.(*Sturm*)/JG 4 and a former bomber pilot, assumed command of II.(*Sturm*)/JG 4 following Kornatzki's death.

RIGHT: An Fw 190 A-8/R2 of 11.(Sturm)/JG 3 in July 1944 showing the additional armour on the sides of the cockpit and canopy. Note the stylised eagle's wing over the exhaust area. This machine, 'Black 13' was flown by Lt. Werner Gerth who, at the end of July, had 19 victories, most of which were four-engined bombers. Although the forward fuselage has been covered over, the engine cowling was all black, as introduced by the Kommandeur, Hptm. Wilhelm Moritz.

Fw 190 A-8/R2 'Black 13' flown by Lt. Werner Gerth of 11.(Sturm)/JG 3 in July 1944

The first Fw 190s delivered to IV.(Sturm)/JG 3 were finished in a standard 74/75/76 factory scheme, but on several aircraft this was subsequently darkened, as shown on this machine where a field-mixed green has been applied over the original camouflage, leaving an area of the original colours around the fuselage Balkenkreuz. The stylised eagle's wing was outlined in yellow on this aircraft and it is thought that the cowling was marked with the badge of JG 3 as shown. Note the slightly oversized Hakenkreuz on the fin.

RIGHT: An Fw 190 A-8/R2 at Schöngau in August 1944. This aircraft, possibly 'Yellow 15', may have been flown by Lt. Oskar Romm, the Staffelkapitän of 15/JG 3. The aircraft has been fitted with additional armour including the so-called Scheuklappen, or 'Blinkers', the armoured glass panels on the canopy sides.

**Emblem of
Stab/JG 300**

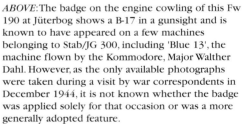

ABOVE: The badge on the engine cowling of this Fw 190 at Jüterbog shows a B-17 in a gunsight and is known to have appeared on a few machines belonging to Stab/JG 300, including 'Blue 13', the machine flown by the Kommodore, Major Walther Dahl. However, as the only available photographs were taken during a visit by war correspondents in December 1944, it is not known whether the badge was applied solely for that occasion or was a more generally adopted feature.

ABOVE RIGHT AND RIGHT: Two views of 'Black 13', a Bf 109 G of JG 53, after a landing accident. In the first photograph showing the machine in the position in which it came to rest, the black unit identification band of JG 53 is clearly visible around the rear fuselage. The second photograph shows the Morane mast under the port wing for the FuG 16ZY as well as the additional damage suffered to the tail unit when the machine was lowered to the ground. Although the photographs are thought to have been taken in the summer of 1944, the name of the pilot and the exact date are not known.

ABOVE: Aircraft of II./JG 300 at Holtzkirchen at the end of August 1944. In the foreground is an Fw 190 A-8/R2 of 7./JG 300, W.Nr. 681366, which was later shot down on 11 September. Note the external armour plate added to the sides of the windscreen and the sides of the cockpit. The fuselage armament has been deleted to offset the increased weight of the armour and improve manoeuvrability.

Focke-Wulf Fw 190 A-8/R2 'White 5' of 7./JG 300, Holzkirchen, late August 1944

This aircraft was finished in a 74/75/76 scheme and the tactical number and Gruppe bar lacked any contrasting outline. The spinner was black with a white spiral and all national markings, with the exception of the upper wing crosses, which were in the white outline style, were black outlined in white.

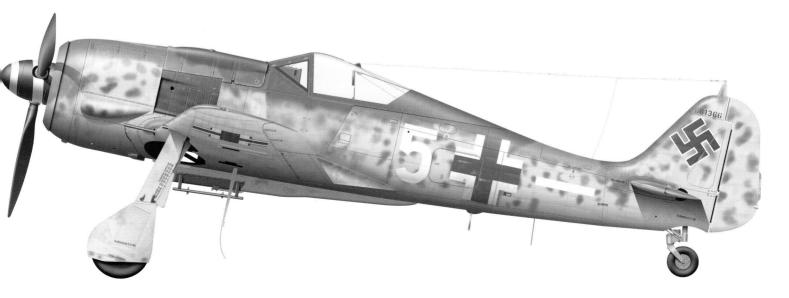

Dark Skies – Autumn/Winter 1944

When Hans-Günter von Kornatzki was killed, his name joined a growing list of experienced fighter pilots and formation leaders who had been lost in action to Allied fighters since the summer. One of the earliest was *Hptm.* Hubert Huppertz, 37-victory *Kommandeur* of III./JG 2 and holder of the *Ritterkreuz* with *Eichenlaube*, who had shot down at least three Allied fighters on D-Day, but who succumbed to the fighter menace himself when he was shot down by P-47s over Caen on 8 June.

On 17 June, after shooting down two Spitfires over the Invasion Front the day before, *Lt.* Anton-Rudolf Piffer, an Austrian of 1./JG 1, was shot down and killed when his Fw 190 was bounced by P-47s near Argentan. With a total of 26 victories which included 19 *Viermots*, he was awarded the *Ritterkreuz* posthumously. On 25 August, *Hptm.* Egon Albrecht of III./JG 76, a former *Zerstörer* pilot born in Brazil, was attacked by US fighters north-west of Creil as he nursed his damaged Bf 109 G-10 home from a patrol. He baled out but was killed in the process. Of his 25 victories, five were *Viermots*. The same day, a fellow former *Zerstörer* pilot, *Lt.* Rudi Dassow, *Staffelführer* of the recently formed 8./JG 6, was shot down in his Fw 190 by a P-38 Lightning near La Fère. He had a total of 22 victories, of which 12 were *Viermots*, and was also awarded the *Ritterkreuz* posthumously.

There were two names which stood out however. On 22 June 1944, *Hptm.* Josef Wurmheller, Huppertz' successor as the *Kommandeur* of III./JG 2 and one of the most accomplished pilots on the Western Front, was killed when he collided with his wingman during combat with Canadian Spitfires near Alencon. He had been awarded the *Eichenlaube* and his 102 victories included at least 20 four-engined bombers and at least 56 Spitfires. He was honoured with the *Schwerten* posthumously.

Then, on 3 September, *Hptm.* Emil Lang, *Gruppenkommandeur* of II./JG 26 was taking off with a malfunctioning Fw 190 A-8 and, after leaving Brussels-Melsbroek in a steep climb with his undercarriage down he was caught by a P-47. The pilot of the P-47, *Lt.* Darrell Cramer of the 338th FS, 55th FG, recalled: "*I was closing very rapidly and the 190 was still in a vertical turn. I throttled back to pick up my lead but was still going too fast, so I could only get to about an 80 percent lead. I fired a short burst from this position from 200 yards. The range was very close and I could distinctly see the crosses on his wings and the egg blue finish on the aircraft. I fired until I was afraid I'd collide with him, so I eased off. As I pulled up for another pass, I saw him upside down. Then he hit and skidded along the ground and burst into flames.*"

Lang is credited with 173 victories of which 144 were over the Eastern Front and 29 in the West (including nine Spitfires, nine P-51s, six P-47s and four P-38s), 28 of which were claimed over the Invasion Front, the highest number of Allied fighters lodged by a German pilot. He had been awarded the *Eichenlaube* to his *Ritterkreuz* in April 1944.

LEFT: This Fw 190 A-8 at Königsberg with the tactical number 'White 21' was flown by Feldwebel Fritz Bucholz of II./JG 6 during conversion training onto the Fw 190. JG 6 was raised from the former Zerstörer unit ZG 26, and the life-sized frontal silhouette of a B-17 painted on the hangar doors was intended to familiarise pilots with the dimensions of the four-engined bomber. The size of the B-17 came as a considerable surprise to many German fighter pilots who were inclined to misjudge the range and open fire too soon.

After Normandy, one by one, the battered fighter *Geschwader* were pulled back into the *Reich* for badly needed rest and refitting; III./JG 1, *Stab*, I. II. and III./JG 2, *Stab*, II. and III./JG 3, II./JG 6, I. and II./JG 11, *Stab*, I., II. and III./JG 26, III./JG 27, *Stab* and II./JG 53, *Stab* and III./JG 76 and I./JG 302.

However, as the *General der Jagdflieger*, Adolf Galland recorded after the war: '*It is characteristic of an air force that to a relatively small group at the front belongs a huge machinery at the rear. It is difficult enough to maintain aggressive strength when advancing, but in a retreat, the weight and bulk of these supporting services have a proportionately negative effect the quicker and more disorganised the retreat becomes.*' It therefore took I./JG 1 ten days to reach its base at Husum, JG 2 was virtually destroyed, III./JG 3 left its airfield in France with Allied armour only five kilometres away and elements of I. and II./JG 26 were attacked as they tried to depart for their designated bases in the *Reich*. By the time JG 1 and JG 11 pulled out of France, they had lost some 100 of their pilots in the fighting there.

Occasionally however, the German Propaganda Ministry could turn to the *Jagdflieger Experten* who had survived thus far; in July, *Major* Josef Priller, *Kommodore* of JG 26 had been awarded the *Schwerten* for his 100th victory on the 18th and *Hptm.* Anton Hackl – soon to take command of the new JG 76 – received the award for his 162nd on the 13th. In August, *Major* Kurt Bühligen, *Kommodore* of JG 2 received the *Schwerten* for reaching 104 victories.

But by the autumn of 1944, intermittent individual accomplishments, no matter how meritorious, did little to salvage the *Luftwaffe's* deteriorating prestige in the eyes of the German leadership. In August 1944, unable to contain his anger any further at the *Jagdwaffe's* perceived abject failure as a fighting force and its evident inability to effectively defend the Homeland against the bombers, Adolf Hitler dragged in its reluctant Commander-in-Chief for a confrontation. For Göring, it was a humiliating experience. In the presence of Generals Jodl and Guderian, Hitler chided: "*The Luftwaffe's doing nothing! It's no longer worthy to be an independent service – and that's your fault!*" The two *Army* generals diplomatically left the room as tears trickled down the *Reichsmarschall's* cheeks.

Despite such a worsening predicament, the Operations Staff of the OKL still saw the *Jagdwaffe's* prime mission in September 1944 as one of air defence and ensuring "... *domination of the air over friendly territory and the destruction of enemy aircraft by day and night.*" In reality however, before domination could be achieved, a more immediate goal was equality, and even on that count the *Jagdwaffe* was substantially outgunned by Allied air strength.

From October through to the end of November, *Luftwaffenkommando West*, the new command established on 22 September to co-ordinate flying operations on the Western Front, reported the following strength figures for day fighters:

	Actual Strength	Effective Strength
2.10.44	343	214
18.10.44	353	191
1.11.44	345	223
28.11.44	494	249

September did see record deliveries of more than 3,000 new or repaired single-engine fighters, largely the results of the *Jägerstab's* efforts. By October new, improved fighter types were reaching the units. III./JG 27, under *Hptm. Dr.* Peter Werfft at Köln-Wahn, took delivery of the first 75 enhanced and aerodynamically refined Messerschmitt Bf 109 K-4s, whilst III./JG 54 under *Ritterkreuzträger Hptm.* Robert Weiss at Oldenburg received the first of the long-nosed Focke-Wulf Fw 190 D-9s in late September, a machine which, powered by the Jumo 213 A engine, would later prove to be an outstandingly manoeuvrable and fast fighter when pitted against Allied types. Despite some initial scepticism on the part of III./JG 54's pilots, within eight days of taking delivery of the D-9, Weiss scored the first victory on the type and his personal

LEFT: After a successful career with JG 54 on the Eastern Front where he accumulated 144 victories, Eichenlaubträger Emil Lang was appointed Staffelkapitän of 9./JG 54 in April 1944. Subsequently his Staffel was transferred to the West and assigned to Defence of the Reich duties, during which Lang increased his tally to 159 victories. On 29 June he then became Kommandeur of II./JG 26 and was credited with another 14 victories, his last being three Spitfires shot down on 26 August. On 29 August the Gruppe transferred from Mons-en-Chausé to Melsbroek but, as a result of British advances in Belgium, was ordered to retreat to Germany. The move began on 3 September but mechanical trouble with Lang's aircraft delayed the take-off of his Stab machines. When they eventually took off, Lang's Fw 190 A-8, 'Green 1', was still giving trouble and he had difficulty retracting his undercarriage. What happened next is still uncertain, but at some point the Focke-Wulfs were attacked by Allied aircraft, probably P-47s of the US 55th Fighter Group, and Lang was shot down, his aircraft diving inverted into the ground.

120th when he shot down an RAF reconnaissance Spitfire south-west of Bremen.

The immediate problem facing the *Jagdwaffe* was a lack of sufficiently trained pilots able to defend the skies over the *Reich* or the Western Front. However, the Western Front had so deteriorated by this stage that neither *Generalfeldmarschall* Model, the *Oberbefehlshaber West*, or his replacement, von Rundstedt, were able to stem the rapid pace of the Allied advance. Virtually unopposed, the troops and armour of the British Second Army broke out of France and swept on into Belgium taking Brussels and the key seaport of Antwerp, its vital harbour installations still intact, in early September. By late October, Montgomery's troops had reached the southern banks of the Scheldt where the task was to flush the estuary of resistance and to open Antwerp to Allied shipping. Worse still, in mid-September and further to the east, the first American troops had crossed the Sauer north of Trier and penetrated the frontier of the *Reich* itself. Two weeks later, elements of the American First Army breached what was thought to be the impenetrable Siegfried Line north of Aachen. The front was collapsing; the Allies were fighting within the borders of the *Reich*.

But from what seemed disaster, *Generalleutnant* Galland was attempting to recover and ultimately mount a reprisal: '...*our fighter units arrived at the Rhine in a chaotic condition. The Gruppen, Geschwadern and even Staffeln had got into a complete mix-up and except for a few, had shrunk to a fifth of their normal strength. It took a long time for the decimated ground crews to find their units. They had sustained great material losses. The existing ground organisations on both sides of the Rhine were in no position to cope with all these new units. Each Luftgau now had additional airstrips under its care. To re-establish order within the Jagdwaffe, we introduced a complete regrouping. My main desire was to create a new reserve...*'

Other *Gruppen*, equally exhausted and only slightly less scathed, returned to the Reich from the Balkans and the East. Elements of JG 302 returned from Rumania and IV./JG 54 and III./JG 11 came in from the East.

Galland: '*Oddly enough, my proposal to give priority to the replenishing and formation of reserves instead of sending forces to the front was accepted without demur by the Supreme Command. As on my two previous attempts in this direction, I maintained that this was the only possible way to deliver the necessary Grosse Schlag – 'Great Blow' – in the defence of the Reich. This phrase was taken up in the highest quarters.*'

With his *Grosse Schlag* policy sanctioned by both Hitler and Göring and the short luxury of a halt in the extended Allied advance, Galland began working to create a reserve of such strength that the *Jagdwaffe* would be in a position to send up at least 2,000 fighters. These would be employed against a single, major raid when, it was envisioned, the bombers could be harried from Sweden to Switzerland and an impact made on the escort fighters. Galland was prepared to sacrifice 400 aircraft and 150 pilots if 400-500 *Viermots* could be brought down in one massive operation. He began by stripping the southern front and Austria of fighters. Such moves meant, for example, that the four *Gruppen* of JG 27 previously scattered across France, Germany and Austria could now be re-consolidated within the *Reich*. The nominal strength of each home defence *Gruppe* was increased as was the amount of specialist training given to pilots serving in the *Reichsverteidigung*. Practice manoeuvres were run through again and again taking into account all possible variations the approach flight the bombers might take and using the lessons gained by I. *Jagdkorps* in the past seven months. Sufficient fuel was scraped together and stockpiled to cover 2,500 sorties and the command infrastructure was revised.

Meanwhile, the challenging regeneration of the *Jagdwaffe* did not entirely distract it from its ability to wage defensive warfare. During September and October, the *Sturmgruppen* were active again. On the morning of 27 September, in what was one of the most formidable missions of its kind, three waves of *Sturmgruppen* numbering some 120 aircraft, escorted by the Bf 109s of I./JG 300, attacked the B-24s of the 2nd Bomb Division whilst on a mission to Kassel. The first wave comprised IV.(*Sturm*)/JG 3 led by *Hptm*. Moritz, the second consisted of II.(*Sturm*)/JG 4 led by *Oblt*. Othmar Zehart and the third wave was II.(*Sturm*)/JG 300 led by *Lt*. Bretschneider. II. (*Sturm*)/JG 4 shot down 26 Liberators of the 445th BG in three minutes – the largest loss suffered by any single USAAF group in one mission in the entire war. German pilot losses from this action amounted to 18 (including Othmar Zehart who is listed as MIA), with a further eight wounded. Thirty-two aircraft were rated as having been 60 per cent damaged or more.

BELOW: Oblt. Othmar Zehart was one of the original cadre of pilots which formed Sturmstaffel 1. An experienced Sturmjäger, he went on to command 7.(Sturm)/JG 4 and on a number of occasions led the whole of II.(Sturm)/JG 4 in the air. Oblt. Zehart was posted missing following a mission against US bombers over the Braunschweig area on 27 September 1944.

The next day, 28 September, the Eighth Air Force bombed an oil target at Magdeburg, but in bad weather only 23 of the 417 bombers found the main target and the rest bombed the city. Of the Fortresses that made it to the target, 27 were from the 303rd BG. They had completed their bomb run and had turned for home when their combat box was attacked from the rear at 12.50 hrs by the Fw 190s of IV.(*Sturm*)/JG 3 which, together with II. (*Sturm*)/JG 4 and II.(*Sturm*)/JG 300, formed a *Gefechtsverband*. The attack was concentrated on the 303rd's Low Squadron and in less than a minute ten bombers were shot down. According to the unit's records: '*Attacks were chiefly from five to seven o'clock, from low to level... The tactics utilized by the enemy pilots demonstrated that they were determined, efficient, and experienced.*'

Lt. Oskar Romm of 15.(*Sturm*)/JG 3 claimed two B-17s for his 84th and 85th victories while *Fw.* Willi Maximowitz, also of 15. *Staffel,* scored his 13th victory. *Fw.* Klaus Neumann of 16.(*Sturm*)/JG 3 shot down his 29th victim and for *Oblt.* Horst Haase, also of 16. *Staffel*, it was another successful mission. B-17 '*Miss Umbragio*'of the 359th BS piloted by Lt. Willam F. Miller suffered hits to two engines and burning fuel streamed out of the ruptured tanks. The tail gunner was killed and his body was still in the wreckage when the aircraft crashed south-east of Wolfenbüttel. The radio operator was blown out of the aircraft, but the rest of the crew managed to bale out. '*Miss Umbragio*' was Horst Haase's 56th victim.

In total, the USAAF lost 34 heavy bombers in the raid with IV.(*Sturm*)/JG 3 accounting for ten of them. An eleventh bomber also failed to make it home. By the end of a month of intensive operations, IV.(*Sturm*)/JG 3 was able only to field some 30 aircraft.

On 15 October, General Doolittle told the RAF that he considered: " ... the German day fighter force was becoming a more and more serious threat." There had been noticeable increases in the numbers of enemy fighters deployed, as well as improvements in tactics and armament.

These were limited successes however, and were not enough to satisfy Hitler. By the end of October, he was again losing patience with what seemed yet more inertia on the part of the *Jagdwaffe*, only this time it was dressed up as 'strategic regeneration'. He had had enough. Still the fighter pilots made excuses; he wanted bombers brought down. On 18 September, a day when the *Jagdwaffe* – unlike USAAF fighters – had flown few sorties due to bad weather, the *Führer* told *Generalleutnant* Werner Kreipe, the *Luftwaffe* Chief-of-Staff, that he thought the *Luftwaffe* was incompetent, cowardly, and was letting him down. What mattered was that the bombers were still getting through, inflicting continual damage to his oil supplies and in this respect he had observed a dangerous new cycle beginning to emerge; despite record aircraft availability, fuel supply was low, which meant that the production plants and refineries were not being protected and, despite Galland's efforts, many pilots had been insufficiently trained due to the lack of fuel!

Göring was prompted to gather a number of his key home defence commanders at the headquarters of *Luftflotte Reich* at Berlin-Wannsee on 26 October to address the problem. Adolf

Galland recalled of this meeting: '*All formation leaders down to and including Gruppenkommandeure were present and a Staffelkapitän from each Gruppe. Apart from that, this glorious speech was also recorded and sent out to the units. It lasted for about three hours. He just kept chewing the same old stuff over and over again; the operations against England and how the fighter escort had not worked properly and then came reproach after reproach – Africa, Sicily, escort missions to Malta, what had the Jagdwaffe achieved in the East? etc... In the end there was doubt cast upon the fighting spirit of the fighters...There were a few who contradicted and they had a very bad time of it... Afterwards, it was so bad that he could no longer bear to look at my face without getting worked up.*'

Then Göring announced: "*I want 500 B-17s brought down next time or I'll have you transferred to the infantry! The Allies know how to put up a good show at fighter protection – use them as an example!*"

At dawn on 2 November 1944, there were nearly 30 operational day fighter *Gruppen* at readiness in Germany with a further 16 refitting or training, totalling 695 aircraft. That day, these units were once again to be tested to their limits. The targets were the refineries at Gelsenkirchen and Castrop-Rauxel and the Leuna hydrogenation plant south-east of Merseburg. Furthermore, Allied commanders were taking no chances on a repeat of the savage punishment their bomber crews had taken over the preceding weeks and had arranged a fighter screen of approximately 600 P-51s.

Despite 9/10ths cloud cover and extremely poor visibility, the *Jagdwaffe* mounted an all-out effort and 500 German fighters were scrambled. Around midday, a *Gefechtsverband* formed around *Hptm.* Moritz's IV.(*Sturm*)/JG 3 and hit the B-17s of the 91st BG in a head-on formation, clawing 13 of the bombers out of the sky. *Ritterkreuzträger Lt.* Werner Gerth was one of 11 pilots from IV.(*Sturm*)/JG 3 killed that day. He had rammed a bomber over Bitterfeld and baled out, but his parachute failed to open. Gerth had 25 four-engined kills to his credit and was a veteran of *Sturmstaffel* 1.

Major Gerhard Michalski led the Fw 190s of II.(*Sturm*)/JG 4 up from Welzow and met the Americans over Köthen. Whilst the Bf 109s of JG 4's escort *Gruppen* took care of the Mustangs, the heavily armoured *Sturmböcke* went for the Fortresses of the 457th BG, sending down nine of them.

The battle raged all afternoon, spreading across Saxony and Thuringia, yet, paradoxically, at the HQ of *Luftflotte Reich*, *Generaloberst* Hans-Jurgen Stumpff was penning a new order to his regional airfield command:

'*The fuel situation makes further restriction of flying operations essential. I therefore issue the following orders:*

1. *A sortie is justifiable only if weather reports and the available tactical information promise success. Those responsible for operations must bear this in mind when issuing operational orders.*
2. *Training flights within units are prohibited until further notice unless specific quotas are issued for the purpose. My approval is required for exceptions to this rule.*
3. *No flights may be undertaken except for operational transfer, test and transport purposes.*'

Meanwhile, *Oberst* Gustav Rödel's JG 27, its four *Gruppen* of Bf 109s operating together for the first time since being brought back into the Reich, tried in vain to get to the bombers but clashed with Mustangs around Leipzig. It was to be the blackest day in the *Geschwader's* history. Fighter after fighter plunged towards the earth and after the battle, JG 27 had suffered no fewer than 38 pilots killed or wounded. Rödel remembered: '*I flew and survived more than 1,000 missions,*

RIGHT: Lt. Klaus Bretschneider, the Staffelkapitän of 5./JG 300, second from the left, with his Fw 190 A-8/R8 'Red 1' in the background. Bretschneider began his career as a Wilde Sau night fighter pilot, in which role he achieved 14 four-engined night victories before transferring to a daylight Sturmgruppe. He then succeeded in destroying several more four-engined bombers and on 7 October shot down one B-17, forced another from its defensive combat box and rammed a third. He was decorated with the German Cross in Gold and received the Knight's Cross on 18 November 1944.

but attacking four-engined bombers flying in formation still remains a nightmare in my memory. Each attack had a different pattern... There were too many odds and unknown factors during an approach, such as weather, the counter-action of the fighter escort and the difficulty in manoeuvring in a large formation. The sole aim of the flight leader was to get his formation into a position which allowed a virtual collision course attack. Thereafter, it was every pilot for himself – he could hardly even keep an eye out for his wingman...'

Figures still differ as to the exact casualties that both sides incurred during the battle, but sources place the Eighth Air Force losses at between 40 and 50 bombers, almost four per cent of the total force, and 16 out of 873 fighters. Galland had lost 120 aircraft and 70 of his pilots with another 28 wounded. The battle had been so severe that Doolittle thought it perfectly reasonable to assume the Germans capable of bringing down up to 100 bombers on any future, deep penetration raid. Writing to Spaatz after the mission, Doolittle warned that as a result of improved, heavier calibre armament, the enemy fighters might soon be in a position to open fire on the bomber boxes beyond the range of their defensive weapons and complained about a shortage of available fighters.

As Galland told an American interrogator in May 1945: *"If the weather from the middle of November and during December had been decent, you might have been attacked by 2,500 to 3,000 fighters. With those numbers, our Fighter Arm would have been in a better position to cope..."*

The *Grosse Schlag* however, had become little more than a pipe dream.

BELOW: A closer view of the inscription below the cockpit shows the lettering and edging with a shadow effect.

ABOVE: An Fw 190 A-8 of II./JG 300 landing at Löbnitz towards the end of 1944. Clearly visible around the rear fuselage is the Geschwader's red, upon which is the black outline of the II. Gruppe horizontal bar.

RIGHT: A line-up of Fw 190 A-8s of 6./JG 300 at Holzkirchen, near Munich, in September 1944, clearly showing the inboard MG 151/20 cannon and the outer MK 108s.

LEFT: This Fw 190 A-8/R2 was flown by Lt. Heimann of II./JG300 and bore the tactical number 'Black 4'.

LEFT: Fw 190 A-8s, possibly of 8./JG 300 at Löbnitz in December 1944.

ABOVE: This Fw 190 D-9 belonged to 7./JG 26 and was used at Reinsehlen in November or December 1944 to train pilots of II./JG 26 converting to the type from their previous Fw 190 A-8s. An unusual feature of this machine, which has a brown horizontal II. Gruppe bar behind the fuselage Balkenkreuz, is the fuselage camouflage which is more mottled than normally seen.

RIGHT: Gefr. Werner Merz of 11./JG 54 in his Fw 190 D-9 'Yellow 4' at Oldenburg in the autumn of 1944. Below the cockpit is the pilot's personal emblem comprising the word 'Bums' in white, meaning a crash or crash-landing, and a green lucky four-leaf clover thinly edged in yellow. Note the early type canopy and head armour.

LEFT AND RIGHT: Oberst Henschel, the local Jagdfliegerführer, or Jafü, decorating Hptm. Julius Meimberg, the Kommandeur of II./JG 53, with the Ritterkreuz at Malmsheim on 24 October 1944. Meimberg was appointed Kommandeur of the Gruppe on 24 April 1944 and remained in command until the end of the war. At the time of the award, he had 45 victories and finished the war with 53.

BELOW AND BOTTOM: Two views of Lt. Hans-Werner Renzow, in peaked field cap, the Staffelkapitän of 10./JG 77, inspecting a Bf 109 K-4 at Neuruppen in November 1944. Although this aircraft, 'White 17', W.Nr. 330230, belonged to 9./JG 77 when shown here, during Operation Bodenplatte it was flown by Uffz. Heinrich Munninger, another pilot of 10. Staffel. Uffz. Munninger carried out an attack but, during the return flight to his base at Dortmund, he was shot down by anti-aircraft fire and killed when his aircraft crashed in flames north-east of Antwerp.

THIS PAGE: Although bearing a close resemblance to the aircraft of Stab/JG 2 in which Fw. Werner Hohenberg was shot down on 1 January 1945, the Fw 190 D-9 shown here at Rhein Main is an entirely different machine, as shown by the position of the Stab markings on the port side of the fuselage in relation to the open hatch and the style of the fuselage cross. These photographs were taken in 1946 and show clearly that the quality of paint used during the closing months of the war fell far below the required standards as laid down by the RLM. Note particularly the erosion of the camouflage on the fuselage and the black of the fuselage Balkenkreuz compared with the paints used for the Stab markings, Hakenkreuz, unit identity bands and that on the engine cowling. The spiral on the spinner consisted of a constant width white line which completed only a single turn and the black Stab markings were thinly edged in white. The identification bands around the rear fuselage are believed to have been black/white/black, indicating that the unit to which this aircraft belonged was JG 4.

withdrawn to Esperstedt to rest and refit. The *Gruppe* then transferred to Bad Lippspringe with 45 Bf 109s, but in return for shooting down 13 US aircraft over the Ardennes, a further 25 of its Bf 109s had been destroyed, 13 damaged, and 15 pilots had been killed and six wounded.

Then, on 31 December, in the company of the *Kommodore Major* Bär, *Major* Langer briefed his pilots and advised them of the forthcoming *Sondereinsatz* planned for the next morning against Eindhoven airfield. The pilots were confined to their quarters at 20.00 hrs and were forbidden to drink alcohol to welcome in the New Year. After a good night's sleep, the pilots were awoken very early the next morning and given a final briefing by *Major* Langer, during which the target, course and attack plan was outlined. Pilots were given specially prepared maps and instructed to make repeated low-level attacks in *Schwärme*.

The *Gruppe's* Bf 109s took off from Lippspringe at 08.25 hrs and were joined by the Fw 190 A-9s of the *Geschwader Stabsschwarm*. The *Gruppe* then assembled with the rest of JG 3 over Lippstadt and set course for Eindhoven. At 09.15 hrs, disaster struck when one of III./JG 3's aircraft flown by *Lt.* Hans-Ulrich Jung, *Kapitän* of 7./JG 3 collided with a power line and his aircraft exploded on the ground. Shock gripped the formation. Soon, however, the *Gruppe* reached the target and, in formation, went in to strafe the airfield which was home to a number of Typhoon, Spitfire and Mustang squadrons as well as some Bostons. As the Messerschmitts swept in, their cannon fire striking fuel and ammunition dumps, fires broke out all over the airfield and personnel ran for cover. Yet amidst it all, some Typhoons attempted to take off and *Lt.* Oskar Zimmermann, *Kapitän* of 9./JG 3 shot down one over the airfield as his 30th victory.

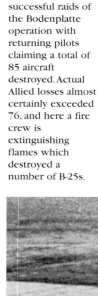

BELOW: The scene at Melsbroek after the airfield had been attacked by JG 27 and IV./JG 54 on 1 January 1945. This attack was one of the more successful raids of the Bodenplatte operation with returning pilots claiming a total of 85 aircraft destroyed. Actual Allied losses almost certainly exceeded 76, and here a fire crew is extinguishing flames which destroyed a number of B-25s.

Another *Staffelkapitän* was lost when *Oblt.* Eberhard Fischler *Graf* von Treuberg, commander of 12./JG 3 and a former member of JG 52 on the Eastern Front with some 20 victories to his credit, was shot down either on the approach to Eindhoven or during the early stages of the attack.

At the end of the mission, around ten Bf 109s of III./JG 3 returned to Lippspringe. The unit War Diary recorded: 'Forming part of a Geschwader strength formation, our Gruppe started with 15 aircraft and was ordered 'to clear' Eindhoven airfield. It would be the last big victory of the Luftwaffe in which Jagdgeschwader 3, destroying 116 aircraft on Eindhoven, had a major part.'

In many cases however, the German formations failed even to find their allocated targets, as with *Obstlt.* Johann Kogler's JG 6 over Volkel, whilst elsewhere they fell as victims of their own Flak or became lost or collided, such as happened to *Major* Gerhard Michalski's JG 4 over Le Culot. In this case, of the 75 aircraft, only around 12, or 15 per cent of the strike force, actually attacked whereas the *Geschwader* suffered a 47 per cent loss rate during the operation. This is comparable to JG 53, which lost 30 Bf 109s out of 80 attacking, or 48 per cent! Recent research indicates that altogether nearly 300 Allied aircraft were destroyed as a result of the raid, of which some 145 were single-engined fighters; another 180 Allied aircraft were damaged and 185 personnel killed or wounded.

Bodenplatte was, without doubt, an unexpected and painful blow for the Allies – particularly with regard to the attack mounted against Eindhoven by *Major* Heinz Bär's JG 3, the attack by II. and III./JG 26 on Brussels-Evere and the strike on Melsbroek by JG 27 and IV./JG 54, but the long-term effect on Allied tactical operations would be negligible. For the increasingly beleaguered *Jagdwaffe* however, the cost was much higher. In total, 143 pilots were killed or reported missing including three *Geschwaderkommodore*, five *Gruppenkommandeure* and 14 *Staffelkapitäne*, with a further 21 pilots wounded and 70 taken prisoner.

LEFT: IV./JG 53 at Stuttgart-Echterdinger was briefed to attack the airfield at Metz-Frescaty. The Gruppe took off but the formation scattered when engaged en route by a US anti-aircraft Battalion. Some aircraft then stayed to engage the AA guns while others continued to attack the briefed target. One of the pilots taking part was Gefr. Alfred Michel of 16./JG 53, who was flying his first operational sortie, but it is doubtful whether he reached Metz. Nevertheless, during the return flight his aircraft was hit by 40 mm shells from the same AA battery strafed earlier by his comrades and his engine stopped. He crash-landed at Waldweistroff, south-west of Merzig, where he was captured after making a brief attempt to escape. So ended Gefr. Michel's one and only war flight and in this photograph he is shown with US personnel examining his Bf 109 G-14, W.Nr. 462892. Although not at all clear in this photograph, the tactical number on Michel's aircraft was apparently 'Blue 2'. Far more obvious despite being partly obscured is the black fuselage band of JG 53, upon which is superimposed a white IV. Gruppe wavy bar.

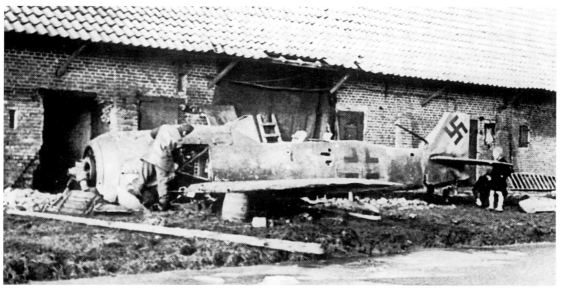

RIGHT 'Red 1', an Fw 190 A-8 of 4./JG 1, after being shot down by anti-aircraft fire on 1 January 1945. The pilot, Uffz. Alfred Frische, crash-landed near Ghent and his machine, W.Nr. 739269, slid for some distance before crashing into a cattle shed. Although badly burned, Frische survived and was taken prisoner.

**Variation of the JG 4
emblem**

Focke-Wulf Fw 190 A-8/R2 'White 11' flown by Gefr. Walter Wagner of 5./JG 4, 1 January 1945

This profile represents the appearance of Gefr. Wagner's before and shortly after it fell into American hands on the morning of 1 January 1945. At that time the badge of JG 4 appeared on the port side of the engine cowling and there was a yellow panel under the nose. The basic camouflage was predominantly a 74/75/76 scheme but with areas around the engine in a badly chipped dark green similar to 83, and with dabs of red primer particularly evident on the external cockpit armour and on the undercarriage doors.

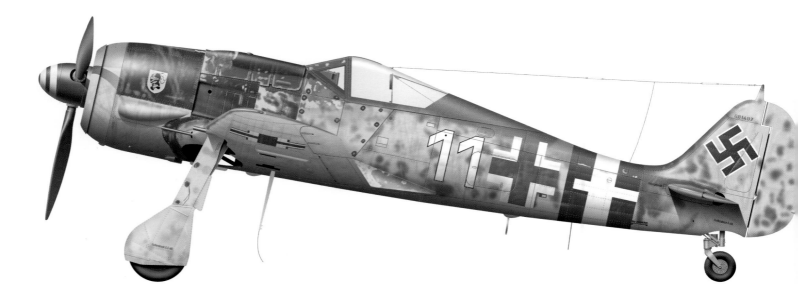

THIS PAGE AND OPPOSITE: During Operation Bodenplatte, the Luftwaffe attack on Allied airfields carried out on 1 January 1945, this aircraft – an Fw. 190 A-8/R2, W.Nr. 681497 – was flown by Gefr. Walter Wagner of 5./JG 4. The Geschwader had been briefed to attack the US Ninth Air Force base at Le Culot and although 75 aircraft of JG 4 took off, Gefr. Wagner and another pilot were delayed and joined up with IV./JG 4. In the event, only about 12 pilots of the Geschwader succeeded in attacking an airfield but they struck nearby St. Trond in error. Wagner, on only his third war flight, had made one pass when his aircraft was hit by anti-aircraft fire and his engine cut out. He was obliged to make an emergency landing south of the airfield where he became a prisoner of war. His aircraft, marked with the tactical number 'White 11' and carrying the knight's helmet badge of JG 4 on the port engine cowling, was subsequently examined by US personnel of the 404th Fighter Group who decided that the aircraft could be restored to flying condition. The views *(OPPOSITE PAGE)* are thought to show the machine shortly after it was acquired by the Americans, at which time it still retained its original engine cowling with Geschwader badge and a yellow lower panel. Note also the dark fillet over the leading part of the wing root which appeared on both sides of the aircraft and that when captured, armoured side panels were fitted to each side of the cockpit. Subsequently, a new engine was located in France and repair work resulted in various changes to the aircraft's appearance. Most noticeable *(THIS PAGE)* is the new engine cowling, now without a yellow underside, and the leading edges of both wings which are either replacement parts or have been stripped during refurbishment.

LEFT: In this view of the starboard side of 'White 11' after the new engine was fitted, one of the armoured side panels fitted to the cockpit sides is clearly visible. These were later removed. Once all work was duly completed, the aircraft was repainted in an overall bright scarlet finish with US insignia and the code OO-L but the machine was never flown again as the tyres had perished and suitable replacements could not be located.

Trouble at the Top

At his headquarters at Berlin-Hottengrund, apparently appalled by the irreplaceable losses inflicted on the *Jagdwaffe* as a result of *Bodenplatte* and aware of the growing plots to oust him from his position as *General der Jagdflieger*, *Generalleutnant* Adolf Galland, prepared himself for the worst. As he recalled: '*It was quite clear to me that only a radical disbanding of our fighter units would ensure the survival of what remained, but this was not an option for discussion. My influence on the Jagdwaffe's further affairs was nil… Before December was out, I approached the Chief of the General Staff (Koller) and asked him to support my request for my return to operational service at the front.*'

This request was ignored. However, between Christmas 1944 and the new year of 1945, during the course of a one-sided, two-and-a-half-hour telephone call, Göring carefully spelt out to Galland the reasons why he would have to go. '*Göring tried to blame me without really having a clear opinion himself,*' Galland recorded in his diary. '*Amongst other things, he reproached me for the following:*

a. A negative influence on fighter tactics
b. A lack of support and failure to enforce orders
c. For having created my own empire in the Jagdwaffe
d. Wrong staff policy
e. Removal of people I did not like
f. My responsibility for the bad state of the Jagdwaffe

'*I was not permitted to say a word in my defence. At the end, Göring expressed his gratitude, saying that after my leave, he would appoint me to an important position within the leadership. I said that this was not acceptable since under no circumstances would I want to be in a leading position now that the Jagdwaffe's collapse was imminent. I again requested to be employed operationally on the Me 262, not as a unit leader, but simply as a pilot. A decision was to be made during my leave.*'

Galland subsequently left for his enforced period of leave '*…embittered, depressed and without any definite plan for the future.*'

The unrest which had been simmering for months within a select group of senior fighter commanders was attributable largely to the increasing levels of abuse being heaped upon the pilots of the *Jagdgeschwader* by their Commander-in-Chief who now regularly threw them into bad-weather operations.

On 30 November 1944, Göring visited the *Stab* of JG 300 at Jüterbog and almost immediately embarked upon an angry confrontation with the *Kommodore*, *Oberstleutnant* Walther Dahl, demanding to know why his unit was not airborne. Dahl replied that adverse weather conditions had prevented the safe take-off and assembly of his formation. Göring

BELOW: Lt. Carl Resch, the Staffelkapitän of 15./JG 54, boarding his Fw 190 A-9 'Yellow 1'. Lt. Resch was flying this aircraft, W.Nr. 205118, on 14 January 1945 when he was hit by return fire from a bomber. He was killed while attempting a crash-landing near Broxten.

BELOW AND BELOW RIGHT: 'Blue 4', a Bf 109 G-14 of 12./JG 53, warming-up its engine at Kirrlach on 13 January 1945. The machine appears to be camouflaged in 74/75/76 scheme.

exploded: *"You cowards! Now I know why your Geschwader holds the record for parachute jumps – you jump so as not to fight! Why have you not obeyed my orders? I shall order my Flak to have you shot from the skies... You and your rotten fighter pilots are going to feel my hand. Before the sun sets tonight, I shall have you shot!"*

However, it was perhaps the humiliating way in which the Galland affair had been handled that provoked outrage, particularly among a group of Germany's finest senior fighter commanders. Headed by *Oberst* Günther Lützow, other officers, including *Obersten* Gustav Rödel, Johannes Steinhoff, Günther von Maltzahn and Hannes Trautloft, were persuaded to rebel against Göring whom, they felt, was being influenced by another clique of ambitious and self-serving personalities. These included *Generalmajor* Dietrich Peltz, the architect of *Bodenplatte*, *Oberst* Hajo Herrmann and *Oberst* Gordon Gollob, themselves all battle-experienced and highly-decorated officers. Throughout January 1945, by means of semi-covert meetings with a number of *Luftwaffe* generals and even SS leaders, the Lützow group attempted to force a confrontation with Göring during which they would put forward their grievances and demand Galland's reinstatement. This proved unsuccessful and on 23 January, Göring officially stated:

'*Generalleutnant Galland has been dismissed from his post following several years service as General der Jagdflieger, in order that he may once again be deployed in command once his health has been restored. I wish to express my sincere thanks to Generalleutnant Galland for his services performed on behalf of myself, for the German Jagdwaffe and for the Fatherland. With untiring zeal in both operations and administration, Galland has fulfilled the aims of the Jagdwaffe.*'

'*In place of Generalleutnant Galland, I have appointed Oberst Gollob to safeguard the duties of the General der Jagdflieger. I expect that the Jagdwaffe will support Oberst Gollob... It should be remembered that it is neither the organisation nor the man that is important, but only the goal that is common to us all – the regaining of air supremacy over German territory.*'

BELOW: The Fw 190 S-8 in this photograph was used by Stab II./JG 301 at Stendal in early 1945 to train pilots transferred from disbanded bomber units. Typical of the period when fuel stocks were dwindling due to the Allied bombing of fuel plants, the aircraft is being towed by oxen. To save fuel, taxiing aircraft under their own power was forbidden and strict penalties were imposed for any unnecessary wastage.

ABOVE: Reichsmarschall Göring (second left) during his visit to Stab/JG 300 at Jüterbog on 30 November 1944. The result was an angry confrontation with the Kommodore, Oberstleutnant Walther Dahl (third from left) and accusations of cowardice.

ABOVE: Two Fw 190 D-9s of 2./JG 26 at Furstenau-bei-Rheine in January 1945. In April, this Staffel provided airfield cover for the Me 262s of NAG 6.

ABOVE AND RIGHT: The II. Gruppe of JG 26 began to receive the Fw 190 D-9 in November 1944 and operated the type until the end of the war, for much of this time operating from Nordhorn in north-west Germany. Close to the airfield was a forest in which the aircraft were concealed from ground-strafing Allied fighters, and here, aircraft of 7./JG 26 are seen on the taxi track which linked the forest with the airfield. The photographs were probably taken in January or February 1945.

The Ta 152

On 2 November 1944, a special test unit designated *Erprobungskommando* 152 was established at Rechlin for developing to operational readiness what many perceived to be the ultimate piston engine fighter, Kurt Tank's Ta 152. The unit was led by the 35-victory *Ritterkreuzträger* and former *Kommandeur* of III./JG 2 and I./JG 11, *Hptm.* Bruno Stolle and was equipped with a small number of Ta 152 H-0 pre-production aircraft all fitted with GM-1 power boost. During early tests, the pilots of the *Kommando* found the aircraft possessed a superb performance, especially at altitude, making it more manoeuvrable than the P-51 Mustang and P-47 Thunderbolt. During one flight, Stolle reached an altitude of 12,000 metres and was only prevented from climbing higher by lack of oxygen.

A plan was then issued on 9 January 1945 to expand the *Kommando* to comprise a *Gruppe Stab*, *Stabskompanie* and five *Staffeln*. However, this was almost immediately abandoned and operational testing was placed in the hands of III./JG 301. Twelve Ta 152s remained with *Erprobungskommando* 152, which was redesignated *Stabsstaffel*/JG 301 on 23 January 1945. Despite this, it remained at Rechlin and was never attached to JG 301. On 9 February 1945 the unit reported a strength of eight Ta 152s, but it is doubtful whether it saw combat.

III./JG 301 had been reformed on 30 September 1944 at Alperstadt from I./JG 302 under the command of *Hptm.* Wilhelm Fulda. Formed in October 1943, JG 301 had been one of the original *Wilde Sau* night fighter units before adapting to all-weather day fighter duties. After operating in Austria, Rumania, Bulgaria and Hungary where its main operations centred on the defence of the oilfields and where it suffered heavy losses, the *Gruppe* returned to the *Reich* for refitting in August 1944 and re-emerged with an establishment of four *Staffeln* equipped, at that time, with the Fw 190 A-8. By January 1945, it had moved to Alteno near Berlin and exchanged its previous equipment for the Fw 190 D-9. The unit was placed under the temporary command of *Hptm.* Karl-Heinz Dietsche pending the arrival of *Major* Guth. One of the unit's pilots at this time was *Fw.* Rudi Driebe of 10./JG 301 who remembered: *"In January 1945 we received about 24 to 26 Ta 152s. Quite a number of these were lost during conversion training due to crash landings and other causes. The remaining Ta 152s were then taken over by the Stabsstaffel of the Geschwader. To my knowledge, only one operation was flown by the Ta 152 at that time. It was during an air raid on Berlin. The Geschwader suffered heavy losses on that day and only the Ta 152s returned safely. If the Ta 152 had seen action a year earlier, things would have looked bad for the P-51."*

In combat it was found that the Ta 152 was inferior to the P-51 in the initial turn but could then tighten its turn and position itself behind the Mustang to bring its guns to bear. The Ta 152 was more sensitive on the controls than the Fw 190 D-9, but possessed a much improved performance, especially at altitude. Another advantage that it had over the Fw 190 that it was much easier to take off and land. One problem that did manifest itself with the H-0 series was that, after retraction, the starboard undercarriage oleo would drop about one third and pilots had to resort to a short diving manoeuvre to lock it in place. This problem was cured on the production Ta 152 H-1.

Fw. Willi Reschke of III. and *Stab*/JG 301 flew the Ta 152 H-1 on 13 March 1945 on a ferry flight from III./JG 301's base at Sachau to Stendal, where the *Geschwaderstab* was based with the Fw 190 D-9s of II. *Gruppe*. A delighted Reschke also happened to be awarded the *Deutsches Kreuz in Gold* from the *Kommodore*, *Obstlt.* Fritz Aufhammer the same day, which coincided with a visit by *Generalleutnant* Dietrich Peltz who was at Stendal to inspect the new fighter. Reschke recalled: *" From 27 January 1945, I only flew the Ta 152 as escort protection for our standard Reichsverteidigung units and I have to say that the later development of the Ta 152 was much superior to all propeller aircraft of the Second World War, but we only had so very few machines in operation. The Ta 152 enjoyed very high climbing ability, very high speed (750 km/h) and a very small turning radius thanks to its larger wing."*

III./JG 301 suffered its first loss on 1 February 1945 when *Uffz.* Hermann Dörr of 12./JG 301 was killed on a training flight near Alteno. Eight days later, *Hptm.* Herbert Eggers lost his life while returning to Tarnewitz in his Ta 152 H-0 following a weapons test at Rechlin.

As the pilots gained experience with the Ta 152, so they became more and more impressed with its capabilities.

BELOW : Generalleutnant Dietrich Peltz, the commander of IX. (J) Fliegerkorps, entering the cockpit of a Ta 152 of 7./JG 301 at Stendal on 13 March 1945. The aircraft was W.Nr. 150007, almost certainly 'Yellow 3', and carried the Geschwader's yellow and red bands around the rear fuselage together with a narrow II. Gruppe bar.

Lt. Hagedorn of 9./JG 301 reported: "*We reached the remarkable altitude of 13,200 metres. Our ground speed, which we later worked out with a Focke-Wulf test pilot, was somewhere between 820 and 830 km/h. I'd never had such a fast aeroplane under me in my life. When you shoved the throttle fully forward, the take-off was incredible. The airfield at Alteno, where I flew it, was 600 metres long. The aircraft took off, and I mean really took off, in 300 to 400 metres! I had never previously seen such a thing, and also above anything I had experienced in any other aircraft was its incredible manoeuvrability. It was known that even a Fw 190 would buffet very easily on the verge of stalling in a dogfight if you pulled too hard. But we noticed in the Ta 152 that you could practically twist it around its tail. The thing really went round. Others experienced aileron snatching but I managed this seemingly impossible turning radius without any problem at all in the ailerons.*"

Although JG 301 suffered one or two losses during the last two months of the war, its Ta 152s claimed a number of victories over both American and Russian fighters. To quote *Lt.* Hagedorn again: "*We often said among ourselves, 'Why didn't we get the Ta 152 earlier?' Among the 'old hares' in our outfit it was always said, 'When we have the thing, we won't be wary of the Spitfire any more.'*"

At the end of April 1945 the *Stabsstaffel* and III./JG 301 transferred to Leck in Schleswig-Holstein where at least two of their Ta 152s were captured by the British Army. These were W.Nr. 150168, 'Green 9' which was test flown in Britain and W.Nr. 150003, 'Green 4' which went to the United States and which possibly was originally marked 'Yellow 4' of 11./JG 301.

LEFT: In February 1945, a member of JG 301 took a number of photographs of the new Ta 152 Hs of 7. Staffel, of which only this one survives. Unfortunately, following an order issued by the Supreme Headquarters Allied Expeditionary Forces on 1 June 1945, which prohibited the wearing of any kind of insignia, medal or decoration marked with the swastika, many ex-servicemen who had served with the German armed forces were so fearful of possible Allied retribution that they disfigured or destroyed anything which they possessed showing a swastika. Some misunderstood the Allied instruction to include photographs, and thus the photographer who took this picture destroyed the rest of his material leaving only this virtually unique image of Ta 152s in service with the Luftwaffe. Note in particular the narrow II. Gruppe bar on the rear fuselage of 'Yellow 1'. The other aircraft parked in the background are 'Yellow 2' and 'Yellow 3'.

Focke-Wulf Ta 152 H 'Yellow 1' of 7./JG 301, Alteno, February 1945
The camouflage finish on Ta 152s was virtually identical to that applied to the later Fw 190 D-9s and consisted of 82 and 83 on the uppersurfaces with 76 below. National markings were the full austerity type overall and on this particular aircraft, the tactical number was angled slightly forward. Note also that the horizontal bar of II. Gruppe was positioned unusually high on the fuselage and that the spinner was plain black.

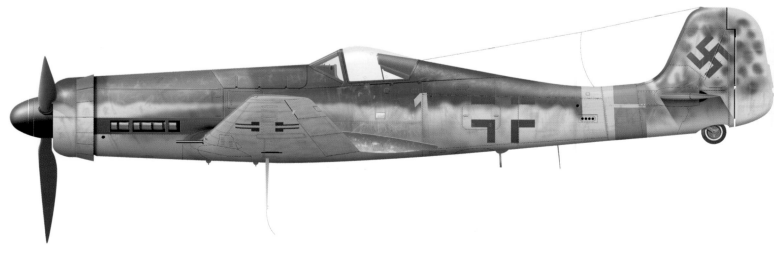

Desperate Times, Desperate Measures – The Final Battles

By February 1945, the rumble of artillery in the East was clearly audible at *Reichsmarschall* Göring's country residence on the Schorfheide, for by now the Soviet winter offensive had formed a critical gap between the two German armies assigned to defend East Prussia. Increasingly desperate, Hitler could only bank on loyalty and tenacity. He therefore gave the task of defending East Prussia to Himmler and his specially-created Army Group Vistula. But already, German troops had evacuated Tannenburg. With nothing to stop it, the Soviet Army had swept across the Oder and successfully established a bridgehead on the western bank. Its advanced units were now only 80 km from Berlin.

Bombs continued to fall on the *Reich*; since the New Year, the Eighth Air Force, working in co-operation with RAF Bomber Command, which was now also bombing regularly by day, had again been systematically hitting the oil refineries. In attempting to intercept the American raids against industrial and fuel targets in northern and central Germany on the 14th, the *Jagdwaffe* lost 107 pilots killed or missing with another 32 wounded, the heaviest casualties being borne over the Elbe and the Havel by JG 300 and JG 301. Tank and aircraft factories, benzol plants and the railway network – marshalling yards, repair shops, junctions, bridges – and also road traffic bottlenecks were subjected to ceaseless attacks by the US tactical air forces. On 22 and 23 January alone, Allied aircraft destroyed 6,000 vehicles as von Rundstedt's battered armies retreated from the Ardennes.

For the *Jagdwaffe*, losses amongst the four *Jagdgeschwader* left for *Reich* defence following a massive transfer of units to the East, were rising to nearly 30 per cent of sorties flown, while victories gained amounted to less than 0.2 per cent of Allied strength. The existing resources were simply not enough, as is illustrated in a situation report issued by the OKL Operations Staff for 3 February 1945 following an attack by 937 USAAF bombers on the Tempelhof marshalling yards:

'*During today's heavy air raid on Berlin, the Reichsmarschall asked the Chief of the Operations Staff why no German fighters were sent up. Owing to the difficulties on the Oder, OKL had ordered that all fighter formations, including those of Luftflotte Reich, be employed on the Eastern Front. These formations were engaged on bombing operations. When the enemy attack on Berlin commenced, JG 301 had already carried out one operation on the Oder Front and JG 300 was bombed-up and ready for a sortie. The Chief of the Operations Staff suggested to the Reichsmarschall that after the enemy bridgehead across the Oder had been eliminated, the fighter formations previously engaged in the Reichsverteidigung as well as further fighter Geschwader used to reinforce Luftflotte 6, be re-assigned to the defence of the Reichsverteidigung. The Reichsmarschall agreed with this proposal. The Chief of Operations Staff will discuss this matter by telephone with the Führer's Luftwaffe adjutant.*'

Such were the odds against the *Luftwaffe* by this stage that during a raid by more than 1,200 Eighth Air Force heavy bombers on a range of oil and rail targets in central Germany on 9 February, the Germans were able to deploy only 67 single-engined fighters. Reviewing this response, the Chief of the Luftwaffe Operations Staff lamented "*...that the employment of such a small number of aircraft is purposeless and must be regarded as a mistake.*"

RIGHT: American B-24 bombers over Salzburg on 27 February 1945. By this stage of the war, it was practically impossible for German fighters to attack the heavily escorted bomber formations and OKL proposed that only lone bombers separated from their formations should be attacked. Note that the defenders have ignited smoke pots to lay a smoke screen.

In late February, with Allied fighters now virtually ruling the skies over Germany, OKL proposed as a measure of survival that German fighters should only attack lone bombers straggling behind a formation.

Although the air war was fast becoming a case of cat and mouse for the Allies, the *Luftwaffe* could still – sporadically – hit back. Throughout late February and March 1945, the fighter units of 14. and 15. *Fliegerdivision,* both of which operated within *Luftwaffenkommando West* and consisted of I., II., and III./JG 2, I., II. and IV./JG 26, I., II., III. and IV./JG 27 and III. and IV./JG 53, carried out regular ground-attack and bombing missions against Allied troops and vehicles as well as artillery-spotting missions and armed reconnaissance around the Rhine and Ruhr areas.

ABOVE: This Fw 190, 'Yellow 7', was flown by Uffz. Karlheinz Kabus of 3./JG 11 who claimed a P-47 as his first victory on 23 December 1944. In January 1944, JG 11 was transferred to the Eastern Front and this photograph, taken at Strausberg in February 1945, shows the machine camouflaged with foliage, tarpaulin covers and netting. Uffz. Kabus finished the war with seven victories, six of which were Soviet aircraft.

On the afternoon of 28 February, 46 Me 109s of III. and IV./JG 53 went out on *Jabo* operations and engaged in low-level combat with 16 P-47s in the Pforzheim area at 2,000-5,000 metres and with eight P-47s over Karlsruhe. JG 53 claimed three P-47s shot down and a probable.

Two days later, II., III., and IV./JG 27 despatched 71 Bf 109s on ground-attack sorties in the Düren, Rheindahlen and Erkelenz areas, as well as acting as escort for 22 Ar 234s of III./KG 76 and 26 Me 262s of II./KG 51 attacking enemy tank and troop concentrations around Düren. JG 27 also engaged RAF Tempests and US P-47s, claiming two of the former shot down for the loss two pilots, although there are no corresponding Tempest or Typhoon losses.

On 5 March, *Gruppen* of JG 26 and JG 27 undertook fighter sweeps in the Duisburg and Düsseldorf areas and a small patrol of Fw 190s of II./JG 26 shot down three artillery spotting aircraft – noted by *Lw.Kdo West* as 'Austers' – in the Krefeld-Urdingen area.

In mid-March the Fw 190 D-9s of *Hptm.* Siegfried Lemke's III./JG 2, operating as part of 16. *Fliegerdivision,* assisted the nocturnal operations of the Ju 87s of NSG 1 and NSG 2, the Fw 190s of NSG 20 and II./KG 200 and the Ar 234s of III./KG 76, by conducting a short campaign in daylight against the bridge across the Rhine at Remagen. From dawn on the 9th until mid-afternoon, formations of up to 24 Focke-Wulfs bombed the bridge. Hits were observed near the central pier and craters were made along the approach road. During these operations, the 'Richthofen' *Geschwader* also encountered six P-51s and engaged in low-level combat, claiming one probable for no losses. At dusk, III./JG 2 sent two Fw 190s to conduct a weather reconnaissance in the Remagen area, but the mission had to be broken off due to bad conditions.

The following afternoon, six Fw 190s took off, each laden with one 250 kg bomb, and, despite ten P-47s defending the target, managed to attack the bridge from 800 metres, scoring one hit on the southern section and one at each end. The *Gruppe* returned between 12.30-13.45 hrs on 12 March sending five Fw 190 D-9s, escorted by aircraft from II./JG 2, on a strafing run. Hits were scored on enemy positions between the pontoon bridge and railway bridge on the west bank. A further 11 aircraft were despatched during the afternoon. There were no casualties.

I. and II./JG 51 and II. and IV./JG 53 also carried out similar repeated attacks against pontoon and railways bridges at Hanau and Mannheim using 250 kg and 500 kg containers of 10 kg fragmentation bombs.

Meanwhile, the war against the bombers was about to reach desperate new heights. Following a request from Göring in early March 1945 for volunteers to take part in a radical operation "...from which there is little possibility of returning", a small group of pilots arrived in great secrecy at Stendal on the 24th to begin training as part of the so-called *Schulungslehrgang 'Elbe,'* known also as *Sonderkommando 'Elbe'.* This was the brainchild of the ever-inventive *Oberst* Hajo Herrmann, the bomber ace who had founded the relatively successful *Wilde Sau* night fighter units in 1943.

Herrmann's plan was to assemble a group of pilots who would be prepared to

BELOW: In March 1945, the training of the volunteers for *Schulungslehrgang 'Elbe'* was organised by the former bomber pilot, Major Otto Köhnke, shown here as a Hauptmann. Köhnke became Kommandeur of II./KG 54 in March 1942 and was awarded the Knight's Cross on 1 August of that year. After being severely wounded and losing a leg, he served with various training units and staffs.

fly their fighters in a massed attack against a large Allied bomber formation using conventional armament but also with the intent of ramming the *Viermots* to bring them down. The chances of survival would be slim, but Herrmann was encouraged by the initial call for volunteers; pilots from JG 1, II./JG 102, II./JG 103, II./JG 104, I./JG 300, II./EJG 1 and even the

ABOVE: On 23 March 1945, attacks by the US Fifteenth Air Force included a raid on the Ruhland oil refineries near Dresden. Taking part in this mission were the B-17s of the 419th Bombardment Squadron, 301st Bombardment Group, which were attacked by a small number of Me 262s from the Geschwaderstab of JG 7. The Americans lost three bombers, one of which was claimed as a probable by Ofw. Gerhard Reinhold and is seen here on fire and dropping out of formation.

Me 163-equipped JG 400 put their names forward and soon Herrmann purportedly had 2,000 names and agreement from Göring that 1,500 fighters – mainly Bf 109 Gs and Ks – would be made available for the operation, which was to be codenamed 'Wehrwolf'.

Herrmann's volunteers were to be trained for their mission by *Major* Otto Köhnke, the former *Kommandeur* of II./KG 54 who had been awarded the *Ritterkreuz* for his actions on the Russian Front in 1942. Köhnke was known to be outspoken and critical of the *Luftwaffe* leadership but blessed with exemplary leadership qualities himself.

Köhnke arranged for the volunteers, many of whom had come from fighter training units, to be briefed by *Ofw.* Willi Maximowitz, a fearless pilot who had flown with *Sturmstaffel* 1 and IV.(*Sturm*)/JG 3 and who had shot down 15 *Viermots*. Further training, which lasted for about ten days, included the showing of morale-boosting films and lectures by political officers on the dangers of Jewish culture and Bolshevism. Indeed, ninety per cent of the training course consisted of political indoctrination with the rest devoted to tactics and operations.

The *Schulungslehrgang 'Elbe'* was to use Bf 109s adapted for the mission by removing the FuG 16Z transmitter and much armour protection, including that around the fuel tanks. In addition, the aircraft armament was reduced to a single, fuselage-mounted MG 131 machine gun with less than 60 rounds of ammunition.

Once weather conditions were favourable enough for a ramming operation, the 'Rammkommando' involved would be provided with high escort and was to make for its respective waiting area in the normal manner and operate under a Divisional VHF commentary. Upon receipt of the code word 'Antreten frei', the ram-fighters were to make for the enemy formation at a height of 1,500 metres above the bombers. The approach was to consist of a long, shallow dive, if possible out of the sun and in line astern. Pilots were to open fire at extreme range and continue firing until the final steep, ramming dive towards a point on the bomber's rear fuselage immediately forward of the tail unit. If possible, the pilot was then to attempt to bale out. Combat with enemy fighters was to be avoided at all costs and pilots were to climb away if attacked.

Finally, at 09.30 hrs on 7 April 1945, the 120 pilots of the 'Raubvögel' Gruppe of Schulungslehrgang 'Elbe' were placed at

RIGHT: In early 1945, Oberst Hajo Herrmann, commander of the 1. Jagddivision, proposed a single large-scale operation using volunteer pilots employed in a ramming attack on an American bomber formation. To succeed, it was estimated that a force of 800 pilots would be required, 400 of whom would need to ram a bomber. It was realised that only 200 of these pilots would be able to bale out after the ramming, but if successful, the operation would strike a blow from which the USAAF would take some weeks to recover. In that time the German oil industry and perhaps also the Luftwaffe's fighter force would be able to stage a recovery. Named 'Wehrwolf', the operation was launched on 7 April 1945 when the US Eighth Air Force sent more than 1,200 B-17s and B-24s, escorted by more than 800 fighters, to attack targets in central Germany. However, far fewer German aircraft were involved than Herrmann had proposed and pilots had received insufficient training. The result was that some 40 Luftwaffe pilots were lost in return for the destruction of only 17 US bombers and five fighters. This photograph shows 'E-Z Goin', a B-17G of the 351st Bombardment Squadron, 100th Bomb Group, which was rammed by a Bf 109 but succeeded in returning to its base at Thorpe Abbotts. The slashes in the tail were made by the fighter's propeller and the panel bearing the serial number was hanging off when the aircraft landed but was pinned in place when the photograph was taken.

30 minutes readiness at Stendal, Gardelegen, Delitzsch and Morlitz. Fw 190s and Ta 152s of JG 301 were to provide escort. With patriotic slogans broadcast into their headsets by a female voice rather than a more useful navigational commentary, the fighters took off. Their target was the 1,261 B-17s and B-24s escorted by 830 fighters out to bomb 16 airfields, ordnance depots, industrial sites and marshalling yards across northern and central Germany.

Immediately after the raid, the Eighth Air Force reported: '... *it appears that this was a desperation attempt on the part of the enemy and although enemy aircraft fought aggressively and made determined efforts to get through to the bombers, our losses were comparatively light... Signs of desperation are evidenced by the fact that Fw 190 pilots deliberately rammed the bombers, baling out before their planes went into the bomber formations and making fanatical attacks through a murderous hail of fire. Tactics were thrown to the wind and attacks were made from all positions, mainly in ones and twos... From today's reaction, it would appear that although the enemy is fighting a losing battle, the German Air Force is preparing to fight to a finish in a fanatical and suicidal manner...*'

Seventeen bombers were lost during the raid, including at least five B-17s from the 3rd Air Division that appeared to have been rammed intentionally. In reality, and allowing for losses caused by Flak, aircraft hit by falling bombs and kills by Me 262 units also operating that day, the destruction of about 12 B-17s was attributable to *Schulungslehrgang 'Elbe'* and recent research indicates that some 40 ram pilots were killed. This equates to a pilot loss rate of 33 per cent, although the Germans lost many more aircraft during the mission. In any event, *Schulungslehrgang 'Elbe'* attempted no further operations.

On 20 April 1945, Adolf Hitler's 56th birthday, the Allies' mounted a heavy daylight raid by more than 800 US bombers against rail targets in the Berlin area. The RAF would follow that night.

Throughout April 1945, fighter operations were generally limited to a continuation of relatively successful support operations for ground forces in western Germany. Strafing and bombing missions against enemy troop concentrations, vehicle columns and bridges around Lüneburg, Magdeburg, Bamberg, and Rastatt were flown by JG 4, JG 26, JG 27, JG 53 and JG 300 in unusually large formations of some 20 or so aircraft. Such operations, however, were on an increasingly less frequent basis.

Now the Soviet Army was only some 16 kilometres from the north-eastern outskirts of the capital and the city shook with the impact of continuous Russian shelling. *Fw. Oskar Bösch*, a veteran of *Sturmstaffel 1* who now flew with 14./JG 3 recalled:

"*The defence of Berlin had now turned to flying against the Soviet Army. On 20 April, my friend Willi Maximowitz disappeared along with four other aircraft over Frankfurt/Oder. His loss to us seemed particularly cruel; we were close to the end. He always carried a machine gun with him because he didn't want to fall into Soviet hands unprepared... Even now, nobody knows what happened to Willi Maximowitz.*

"*On 24 April 1945 it was my turn. That day, I had just landed at Prenzlau after escorting two Me 109 G-8s on a photo-reconnaissance when I saw a formation of Il-2s flying towards our airfield. Without orders, I took off with my comrades to catch them. In minutes we were attacked by the Soviet escort. This turned out to be tough. I had time to reach the clouds through the Yak fighters. I had the feeling that I was playing with my own life. Everywhere there were Soviet fighters. Taking advantage of a moment of relief, I decided to attack a flight of Il-2s, but could not stay unnoticed for long enough and had to move rapidly from cloud to cloud. As I noticed that my flight was taking me further to the east, my control ordered me back to Prenzlau. As I flew west, I was attacked head-on by one of four Yak-9 fighters. I opened fire at him; seconds later I collided with my attacker! How I managed to parachute from the wreckage, I'll never know. I landed in the Russian front line surrounded by hundreds of Red Army soldiers. With their weapons pointed at me and their hateful looks, I realised that these were my final moments. Luckily, a political commissar intervened to question me. I was limping badly, but got no sympathy from my captors who were content to push me along towards their trenches.*

BELOW: This Fw 190 D-9 was apparently shot down by a US fighter on 3 April 1945 although the pilot succeeded in making a safe emergency landing in farmland. The unit to which the aircraft belonged has not been positively identified although it was probably not from either JG 26 or JG 54 since, as far as is known, neither unit lost any aircraft on 3 April. It is possible that the light area on the rear fuselage may be the yellow/white/yellow identification bands of JG 2.

On the way, I saw a large piece of metal which I recognised as part of the undercarriage from my plane and other debris from the Russian fighter.

"The following three days were dreadful. I escaped on 27 April from the Garz/Oder camp and made my way to Bodensee, some 1,000 km away. This I managed hungry and with an injured knee. I found that this backed up our motto of, 'What can't kill us, can only toughen us!'"

By 28 April, the *Jagdwaffe* was in a state of systematic disbandment and collapse. That day, the *Kommodore* of JG 51, *Major* Heinz Lange, met with *Obstlt.* Karl-Gottfried Nordmann, the *Inspekteur der Jagdflieger Ost and Jafü Nord Ost*, to arrange the disbandment of his *Geschwader*. JG 51, of which Nordmann had earlier been *Kommodore*, had taken part in the air defence of Berlin and in three weeks had, according to Lange, achieved a remarkable 115 victories for five losses. After his meeting, Lange returned by train to his *Geschwaderstab* at Garz and ordered II./JG 51, based further south, to be disbanded. The I. and III./JG 51 under *Hptm.* Joachim Brendel with Bf 109s were still at Junkertroylhof in East Prussia, and on 15 April, Lange flew there in his Fw 190 to make what would probably be a final inspection of the *Gruppen*. On 24 April he returned to his *Geschwaderstab* only to move again three days later to Schmoldow. The following day, the *Geschwaderstab* of JG 51 and the Signals Company were disbanded, effectively leaving *Oblt.* Günther Josten's IV./JG 51 as the only functioning *Gruppe*. This unit, now operating a small number of Fw 190 D-9s, had within its ranks one *Eichenlaubträger*, *Oblt.* Josten (with JG 51 since 1942, 420 missions and 178 victories) and no fewer than six *Ritterkreuzträger* – Lange, *Lt.* Kurt Tanzer, *Kapitän* of 13./JG 51, (723 missions) and approximately 128 victories), *Oblt.* Bernhard Vechtel, *Kapitän* of 14./JG 51, (860 missions and 108 victories), *Oblt.* Anton Lindner, *Kapitän* of 15./JG 51, (650 missions and approximately 73 victories), *Ofw.* Heinz Marquardt, 15./JG 51, (320 missions) and *Ofw.* Helmut Schönfelder (540 missions, 56 victories). On 29 April, *Major* Lange and *Ofw.* Alfred Rauch, another JG 51 *Ritterkreuzträger* with 60 victories, encountered four Soviet La 7 fighters over Neubrandenburg while flying from Schmoldow to Neuenlübke. Rauch shot down one and in so doing scored the last victory of the war for *Jagdgeschwader 51 'Mölders'*.

On 1 May, British forces under Field Marshal Montgomery continued their drive across northern Germany and advanced from the Elbe towards Berlin virtually unopposed. Adolf Hitler had just committed suicide in Berlin, where there was now street-fighting with the Russians, and Hermann Göring was under house arrest in southern Germany for attempting to seize control of what remained of the Third Reich as a result of the *Führer's* self-imposed incarceration. In the air, the *Jagdwaffe* continued its last, spasmodic but defiant defensive operations on the Western and Eastern fronts. During the late morning, a formation of six Fw 190 D-9s of 15./JG 51 under the command of 23-year-old *Ofw.* Heinz Marquardt took off from Parchim to escort a formation of ground-attack aircraft to Berlin. In an operational career that spanned

ABOVE: An Fw 190 A-9 of II.(Sturm)/JG 4 photographed in a wooded dispersal, probably at Delitzsch or Mörtitz, in early 1945. The aircraft has been newly delivered and its tactical markings have yet to be applied.

BELOW: Two *Ritterkreuzträger* of IV./JG 51 photographed at Parchim in late April 1945. On the left is Lt. Kurt Tanzer, the Kapitän of 13./JG 51, while on the right is Ofw. Heinz Marquardt of 15./JG 51. By the end of the war, these two pilots between them had flown more than 1,000 missions and shot down a total of 249 enemy aircraft.

BELOW: Major Heinz Lange (centre), the last Kommodore of JG 51, photographed during a visit to Parchim airfield in late April 1945. Awarded the Ritterkreuz on 18 November 1944, Lange claimed no fewer than 24 Russian Il-2s shot down in the East. His final victory score was 70.

ABOVE: Increasingly towards the end of the war the Luftwaffe suffered heavy losses of aircraft on the ground as a result of low-level Allied strafing. This resulted in German aircraft being carefully concealed and in this photograph, a Bf 109 K-4 of 11./JG 53 is seen taxiing from its wooded dispersal area in April 1945. Just visible are the characteristic outer undercarriage doors of this version.

320 Bf 109 and Fw 190 fighter missions flown with IV./JG 51, Heinz Marquardt was credited with 121 confirmed and 16 unconfirmed victories, all scored on the Eastern Front. His tally included 77 Russian fighters, 24 twin-engined medium bombers and 20 Il-2s *Shturmoviks,* and on 7 October 1944, he downed eight enemy aircraft in one day. He was himself shot down seven times and awarded the *Ritterkreuz* in November 1944.

Having concluded their mission which was intended to be the unit's last operation before surrendering to Allied forces, the *Doras* returned with the fighter-bombers to Schwerin. At 13.00 hrs, as they commenced their approach to the airfield, the German formation was spotted by six RAF Spitfire XIVs from 41 Sqn which had been detailed to conduct a sweep around Schwerin Lake and the neighbouring airfield. Two of the Spitfire pilots, F/L Peter Cowell and F/O Walter Jallands, climbed to 6,000 ft, turned back over Lake Schwerin and observed '... *two long-nosed Fw 190s flying east at zero feet over the water.*' They then dived and chased the D-9s across the lake with Cowell opening fire from 300 yards on the right-hand Focke-Wulf. The German fighters broke away in opposite directions, Marquardt turning sharply to the right while his wingman, *Fw.* Heinz Radlauer, banked left. Cowell closed to 50 yards, his guns registering hits on the cockpit of Marquardt's aircraft. Injured in the head, Marquardt fell forward, smashing his nose on his gunsight, and his Focke-Wulf climbed almost vertically, streamed black smoke, flipped over and crashed close to the lake. Marquardt, however, had succeeded in baling out and landed in the grounds of a nearby hospital, where he was found hanging half-conscious from his parachute outside a window of a nurses' home. The nurses managed to haul him in through the window, and as Heinz Radlauer later recalled: "... *that was the end of his war!*"

Cowell also attacked another Fw 190 during this engagement which was seen orbiting to the north. The pilot of this aircraft also baled out and the aircraft crashed on the south-eastern shore of the lake. Meanwhile, *Fw.* Radlauer, an experienced 100-mission Eastern Front *Jagdflieger* with 15 victories, was pursued towards Flensburg at tree-top height by another Spitfire, but was able to outrun his pursuer and escaped. Commenting on this engagement, the war diary of IV./JG 51 stated:

'*Against destiny we are all helpless... This was shown on 1 May when our Ofw. Marquardt – honoured and recognised by the Gruppe as being one of our finest fighter pilots – was shot down by a Spitfire over Schwerin during the last mission of the war...*'

Five days later, on 6 May 1945, a party of four British Air Disarmament Officers and personnel from the RAF Regiment drove from the headquarters of Montgomery's 21st Army Group at Lüneburg to accept the surrender of *Luftflotte Reich* from *Generaloberst* Hans-Jürgen Stumpff at Schleswig. A British record of subsequent events reads:

'*The Headquarters of Luftflotte Reich was situated in the middle of the thick, dark pine wood at Missunde, about six-and-a-half miles east of Schleswig town, and in this wood the various caravans and trailers were scattered, very heavily camouflaged, notwithstanding the fact that it was quite impossible to see anything through a wood of such density. We were led to a very comfortable caravan and found Colonel General Stumpff waiting outside to receive us. He made no attempt to shake hands, but*

BELOW: Alarmstart! Lt. Günther Landt, the Staffelkapitän of 11./JG 53, taking off in a Bf 109 K-4 with the tactical number 'Yellow 14'.

BELOW: Aircraft were often hidden some distance away from the take-off area and here another Bf 109 K-4 of 11./JG 53 is seen as it taxies from its dispersal onto the airfield to take off.

saluted and the salute was returned; we were led very courteously and correctly into the caravan where the various senior officers of the staff were presented. Fortunately, only one of them, the Chief of Staff, offered to shake hands – a very difficult gesture to refuse, but this hurdle was successfully avoided. The C-in-C pleaded lack of communications – a fact which was well understood – and said that he hoped to have news of the whereabouts of all his units within the next 48 hours. We had the impression that he was somewhat ashamed at being so disorganised, and it was quite clear that he wished to straighten out his difficulty and get his units under control as soon as possible.'

The following day, in a small schoolhouse at General Eisenhower's headquarters in Reims, *Admiral* Hans-Georg von Friedeburg and *Generaloberst* Alfred Jodl, representing *Admiral* Karl Dönitz, Hitler's successor, signed the terms of the German capitulation.

ABOVE: Lt. Günther Landt of 11./JG 53. Landt joined 8./JG 53 in 1942 but did not claim his first victory, a Spitfire in Tunisia, until 5 May 1943. He remained with the Staffel and in August 1944, when it was redesignated and became 11./JG 53, he became Staffelkapitän. Landt survived the war with 23 victories including one in the East and one B-24 four-engined bomber.

BELOW AND BOTTOM: In late December 1944, III./JG 54 was placed under the command of JG 26 until 25 February 1945 when its 9., 10. and 11. Staffeln were officially redesignated 15./JG 26, 13./JG 26 and 11./JG 26 respectively to form IV./JG 26. At about the same time, a new III./JG 54 was formed at Grossenhain from the Zerstörer unit II./ZG 76. This Fw 190 A-8 'Black 15' of 10./JG 54 (previously 5./ZG 76) was damaged by gunfire in March 1945 and its pilot, Fw. Heinz Schmidt, was obliged to make a wheels-up landing at Müncheberg, Berlin. The purpose of the white stripe, which also appeared on the tails of some other aircraft of the reconstituted III./JG 54, is unclear but one as yet unproven theory is that it was used by units which fought in the defence of the Oder River. The new III./JG 54 was certainly so engaged in late February and March 1945 before being disbanded in April. Another equally plausible possibility was that it was a device to help aircraft from the Gruppe remain together in the air, particularly in poor visibility, and acted rather like the formation-keeping strip lights on modern military aircraft.

ABOVE: On 1 May 1945, Fw. Heinz Radlauer of 15./JG 51 flew as wingman to Ofw. Heinz Marquardt in what would prove to be III./JG 51's final mission and, indeed, one of the Luftwaffe's last fighter missions of the war. Radlauer was an experienced fighter pilot with 15 victories, which included four Shturmoviks and two Yak 3s shot down in one mission two weeks earlier.

THIS PAGE: Although briefed to attack Volkel airfield during Bodenplatte, the majority of aircraft which took off on 1 January 1945 failed to locate the target due to a navigational error. Instead, other airfields were attacked by mistake but the operation cost JG 6 a total of 28 aircraft shot down with others damaged and 23 pilots killed, missing or taken PoW. One of the casualties was the Kommodore, Obstlt. Johann Kogler, *(LEFT)* whose Fw 190 D-9 was hit by anti-aircraft fire. After making an emergency landing close to the minor airstrip which he had attacked instead of Volkel, he was taken prisoner with slight injuries. Soon after Bodenplatte, the Geschwader moved to the Eastern Front and on 16 January, Kogler was replaced by Major Gerhard Barkhorn *(RIGHT)*. Although Barkhorn had achieved his 301st victory on 5 January, he had still not completely recovered from wounds sustained in May 1944 and would not achieve any further victories. By this time, the unit had received examples of the Fw 190 D-9, and although Barkhorn *(BELOW)* is known to have flown this aircraft, he was much more familiar with the Bf 109 G which he preferred and continued to fly. In the event, Major Barkhorn only remained with JG 6 until March when he left to seek medical treatment and convalescence [1]. Very few photographs of Major Barkhorn's Fw 190 D-9 are available and none show the complete aircraft. Standing on the wing *(BELOW RIGHT)* is Albert Kustner who served as Barkhorn's chief mechanic for some considerable time.

Focke-Wulf Fw 190 D-9 flown by Major Gerhard Barkhorn, Kommodore of JG 6, February 1945

As very few photographs of Major Barkhorn's Fw 190 D-9 exist, some of the details in this profile cannot be confirmed although the Stab markings and the name 'Christl' on the fuselage are known to be accurate. The aircraft is depicted here with uppersurfaces in 82 and 83 and undersurfaces in 76. The spinner is shown with a white spiral and although JG 6 was allocated red/white/red rear fuselage bands, the need for these had largely ceased by February 1945 and were probably not applied to this aircraft.

1. For more details of Gerhard Barkhorn's military career, together with other photographs of his Fw 190 D-9, see the short biography in 'Jagdwaffe', Volume Five, Section 2.

ABOVE: This Fw 190 D-9, 'Yellow 8', W.Nr. 600375, was found abandoned on an airfield near Celle in late March 1945 by members of 80 Sqn. This machine originally flew with 11./JG 26 and may simply have been abandoned or transferred to another part of the Geschwader when the III. Gruppe was disbanded on 23 March 1945. The shattered propeller on an otherwise apparently undamaged aircraft suggests a taxiing accident.

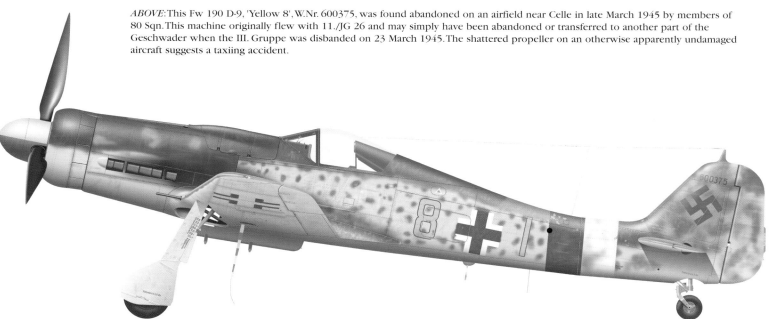

Focke-Wulf Fw 190 D-9 'Yellow 8' of II./JG 26, Celle, March 1945
This aircraft is depicted in an 82/83/76 camouflage scheme and with the black and white unit identification bands of JG 26 around the rear fuselage. Note the small mottles on the fuselage sides and that the spinner was half white and half black with a hard dividing line. Although shown here with the undersurfaces of the wings painted 76, it is possible that these areas were only partly painted and that some areas remained natural metal. Note that this profile represents the aircraft in flying condition and not in the damaged state as photographed.

RIGHT: When two pilots from 5./JG 26 were transferred to NAG 6 at Lechfeld in April 1945, they took their Fw 190 D-9s with them and this machine, 'White 10', photographed at Schleswig after the surrender, is believed to show one of them. Although the Werknummer on the tail is unclear, it may have been 211118, and the machine is believed to have been camouflaged in 82 and 83 on the uppersurfaces and 76 on the undersurfaces. Note, however, that the lower part of the undercarriage door may be natural metal.

ABOVE: Despite the difficulty in interpreting colours from monochrome photographs, the identification bands and the presentation of the II. Gruppe horizontal bar on this aircraft are perfectly consistent with JG 2. It is thought, therefore, that when this Geschwader began converting from the Bf 109 G to the Fw 190 D-9 in December 1944, this particular aircraft, a Bf 109 G-10, 'Black 4', W.Nr. 150816, which was captured at Langensalza in April 1945, had already been passed to another unit. However, as there is no evidence of an earlier tactical number being painted out, the machine may have been used by an unknown unit with its original markings or may still have been in the process of being refurbished when it was abandoned.

Messerschmitt Bf 109 G-10 'Black 4', ex-II./JG 2, Langensalza, April 1945
This aircraft was finished in a 74/75/76 grey scheme with all national markings except the swastika in the austere, outline style. The spinner decoration, which also served as a recognition feature, was in black and white and, similarly, the tactical number '4' was black, edged in white. A small II. Gruppe bar was superimposed upon the yellow and white bands around the rear fuselage.

RIGHT: It became common practice in 1944 to roughly spray the last digits of the aircraft's Werknummer on the rear fuselage to identify it during ferry flights.

THIS PAGE: This Fw 190 A-9 'Red 22' was photographed at Langensalza in April 1945. All national markings were in the maximum simplified style and the red tactical number, together with the red and yellow unit identification bands around the rear fuselage, indicate that the machine had flown with 6./JG 301. Note that parts of the fabric have been cut away from the starboard side of the rudder, suggesting that this machine may have carried two rows of victory markings which, although extremely rare in the closing months of the war, was not entirely unknown.

Focke-Wulf Fw 190 A-9 'Red 22' of 6./JG 301, Langensalza, April 1945
Although this Aslau-built Fw 190 A-9, W.Nr. 490044, was completed in December 1944 or January 1945, it was still finished in the 74/75/76 camouflage colours but all national markings were in the austere style. Note how the typically thin red Gruppe bar used by II./JG 301 had been presented to make it visible against the red of the unit identification band.

RIGHT: A large number of German pilots also decided to fly to the West and, either by design or navigational errors, a total of seven Fw 190s landed in Sweden. The pilot of this Fw 190 A-8, W.Nr. 961076 with the tactical number 'Black 10', was Obgfr. Aksel-Meinhard Kessler, an Estonian pilot flying with 6.(Sturm)/JG 4, who decided not to await the end of the war and landed at Bullofta in the morning of 19 April 1945. Post-war, Kessler emigrated to the United States. His aircraft was armed with four MG 151/20 cannon in the wings.

Focke-Wulf Fw 190 A-8 'Black 10' flown by Obgfr. Aksel-Meinhard Kessler of 6.(Sturm)/JG 4, April 1945

The uppersurfaces of Obgfr. Kessler's machine were camouflaged in 75 and 83 with some freshly repainted areas of 83, particularly on the forward fuselage. Undersurfaces were 76, and the original black/white/black unit identification bands around the rear fuselage had been overpainted, the area above the II. Gruppe bar being in solid 02 while, curiously, that below the bar more closely matched the fuselage finish. The spinner was black with a white spiral, and part of the fairing from the ETC 501 rack under the fuselage was missing, revealing the wiring and parts of the internal structure. The dark mark at the bottom of the undercarriage door was probably engine oil deposited in flight when the undercarriage was in the retracted position.

ABOVE: Another aircraft which landed at Bullofta before the end of the war was 'White 15', an Fw 190 A-8 W.Nr. 739136 of II.(Sturm)/JG4. It was flown by Estonian pilot Oblt. Anatol Rebane who took off from Parchim, north-west of Berlin, on 30 April. Unlike a number of other defectors who were interned in Sweden and subsequently handed over to the Soviets, Rebane lived in Western Europe and the United States after the war but returned to his homeland in 2002.

THIS PAGE: The camouflage and markings on this captured Bf 109 G-14/AS shown at Kassel in 1945 include several interesting features which in many ways are typical for the period. The numbers 6316 on the rear fuselage are the last four digits of the Werknummer and were applied in this fashion to identify the machine during ferry flights. Whereas previously it had been the practice to assign a ferry number completely unconnected with the aircraft's Werknummer, in the later stages of the war, when it became necessary to save time and improve efficiency, it was decided to apply the last part of the aircraft's Werknummer to the rear fuselage for this purpose. In many cases, this was roughly sprayed (see photograph at bottom of page 82), but on this machine it has clearly been applied with the aid of a stencil. At this time, too, following the dispersal of the German aircraft industry, components were arriving at the assembly plants from various sub-contractors. Since many of these components arrived already camouflaged, assembly often resulted in mismatching and, where this tended to compromise the camouflage effect, some respraying was necessary. This practice may be seen on this machine where the roughly sprayed patches of 76 on the vertical tail unit were intended to blend the dark 81/83 colours with the camouflage on the rest of the airframe. That the aircraft eventually served with a front-line unit is confirmed by the tactical number 'White 4' on the fuselage. Concerning the full Werknummer, known Bf 109 G-14 Werknummer blocks indicate the full serial of this aircraft may have been 166316 or 786316.

Messerschmitt Bf 109 G-14/AS 'White 4', unknown unit, Kassel, 1945

'White 4' was camouflaged with 75 and 83 on the uppersurfaces and 76 on the fuselage sides and all undersurfaces. The fin and rudder, being manufactured by a separate sub-contractor, were in 81 and 83 with the latter oversprayed with 76. Note also the other signs of sub-contracted components around the tail area, particularly under the tailplane, and how, after assembly, a thin, irregular band of 76 had been applied to the rear fuselage to adjust the demarcation line between the upper and undersurface colours.

LEFT: While many German aircraft were scrapped at the end of hostilities, some examples were selected for preservation and the machines assembled here were photographed at Eggebek in the British zone of occupation prior to shipment to Britain. In the foreground is a Bf 109 G-14, W.Nr. 464863, with the black tactical number '863' edged in white. Apart from this unusually high tactical number, which indicates that the aircraft belonged to a Luftwaffe training unit, it was not normally applied so far forward on the fuselage. Although the machine arrived in Britain as planned, its fate after about February 1950 is not known.

BELOW: Various Fw 190s of IV./JG 51 at Flensburg in May 1945. Note the white diagonal stripe over the swastika on the Fw 190 A-8 'White 5' of 13./JG 51 to the left of the picture, the significance of which is not known for certain. The machine in the centre of the photograph is an Fw 190 D-9, 'White 11', W.Nr. 213097, which also flew with 13./JG 51. Clearly visible is the outline style Balkenkreuz on the fuselage in black and the white wavy IV. Gruppe bar. Note also the apparently unpainted cover over the fuselage-mounted MG 131 machine guns.

Focke-Wulf Fw 190 D-9 'White 11' of 13./JG 51, Flensburg, May 1945

'White 11' was predominantly finished in 82 and 83 on the uppersurfaces with 76 on the undersurfaces, but the panel covering the machine guns in the fuselage was natural metal. The spinner was plain 70 and had no white spiral, and a light overspray of one of the two uppersurface greens was applied to the lower part of the undercarriage fairings. Other photographs, not reproduced here, of the tail area of this machine confirm that the Werknummer was 213097, as shown in the profile. The finish aft of the Gruppe marking may indicate that the machine had previously belonged to a unit which employed a unit identification band.

Focke-Wulf Fw 190 D-9 'Black 1' of 6./JG 26, Lister, May 1945

'Black 1, W.Nr. 210972, was finished in 75 and 83 on the uppersurfaces with 76 on all undersurfaces and, although not visible in the reference photograph, the spinner is believed to have been black with a white spiral, as shown, but may have been plain black or green 70. Note the MW50 inverted triangle on the fuselage and that the panel surrounding the exhaust, shown here with a heavy carbon deposit, was painted black. Beneath the fuselage is a 300 litre auxiliary fuel tank of a new design which was only produced in limited numbers before the end of the war and did not therefore see widespread use.

LEFT: On 5 May 1945, II./JG 26, then based at Husem, was ordered to fly to Lister in Norway. One of the pilots who made this flight was Fw. Gerhard Müller-Berneck of the 5. Staffel and a former reconnaissance pilot, who flew this Fw 190 D-9, 'Black 1, W.Nr. 210972, which actually belonged to 6./JG 26. The following morning, Fw. Müller-Berneck flew this aircraft back to Germany and landed near Bayreuth in Bavaria where he surrendered to US forces.

LEFT: Two Fw 190s, a Ju 188 and a Ju 88 night fighter on an airfield occupied by US forces at the end of the war. Unfortunately, neither the unit to which the Fw 190s belonged nor the location are known. The simplified type of national markings on the Fw 190 nearest the camera, 'Red 10', would suggest that this is a late production aircraft but it nevertheless shows a surprisingly bright blue undersurface colour on the undercarriage doors, the cowling and the area upon which the tactical number has been placed.

ABOVE: In this view of various aircraft abandoned at Prien in Germany in May 1945, the Bf 109 G-10 with the tactical marking 'Black 11' is a Bf 109 G-10 with the W.Nr. 770184 or, perhaps, 770134. The Fw 190, probably an A-8, has the tactical number '19' and II. Gruppe bar, both probably in red outlined yellow. An area of paint under the '9' shows that the aircraft's markings have been changed at some time. The position of the fuselage band on this machine is unusual and its colour difficult to determine. If it was intended to be a unit identification band, it may indicate that the machine belonged to JG 3 if white, or to JG 11 if yellow.

LEFT: Among the various aircraft of all types found by the Allies on Wunstorf airfield in May 1945 were at least 28 Bf 109 G-6s, G-10s and G-14s plus two K-4s. One, W.Nr. 332700, was burnt out, while this machine, reported as W.Nr. 330255, was intact although it had made a crash-landing and had been looted. It had been flown by the Adjutant of III./JG 27 and was marked with a single black chevron edged in white with a similar vertical bar on the wide green unit identification band around the rear fuselage.

Messerschmitt Bf 109 K-4 flown by the Gruppenadjutant of III./JG 27, Wunstorf, May 1945

The camouflage on this aircraft was typical of that applied to Bf 109 K-4s with Werknummern beginning with 330 and mainly consisted of 75 and 83 on the uppersurfaces with 76 on the undersurfaces. On the fuselage and the leading edges of the wings, the upper and lower colours were separated by an undulating demarcation line. The fuselage had been extensively oversprayed, probably with a light application of 83, which also included the white areas of the fuselage Balkenkreuz. The fin was painted 83 and 81 and the rudder was 75 with hard-edged patches of 83, evidently applied with the aid of a stencil. Although RAF A.I.2 (g) Report No. 269 dated 12 May 1945 states that the Werknummer was 330255, this did not appear on the aircraft. Other markings comprised a neatly applied and well-proportioned black and white spiral on the spinner and the green fuselage band of JG 27. Note that while part of the swastika on the port side of the fin had either been oversprayed or had faded, that on the starboard side was intact.

THIS PAGE: This Bf 109 G-14/AS, W.Nr. 784930, found by Allied forces in 1945, had the tactical number 'Green 1' and the green and white unit identification bands allocated to JG 77. The Werknummer appeared on the tail in black and the spinner was decorated with a white spiral. The overall uppersurface scheme appears to be 75 and 83, but note the typically mismatched finish on the rudder and that the dark areas of 81 and 83 above the 76 at the base have been oversprayed with mottles of 76 in a deliberate attempt to lighten them. The lack of a Gruppe bar on the rear fuselage indicates this machine was probably flown by JG 77's I. Gruppe.

Messerschmitt Bf 109 G-14/AS 'Green 1' of I./JG 77, 1945

Although the cowling of this aircraft was missing when photographed, this profile is believed to be a reasonably accurate representation of how the complete aircraft may have appeared. The inclusion of the 'Herz As' badge is based upon other late-war photographs of aircraft from this unit showing that JG 77 was one of the few units which continued the tradition of unit heraldry virtually until the end. The overall camouflage scheme is shown as 75/83/76, but note the rudder is 81 and 83 oversprayed with 76.

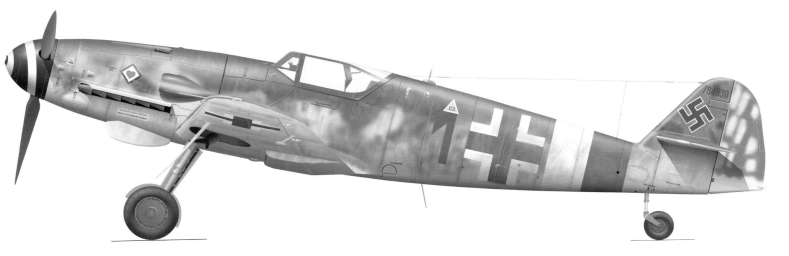

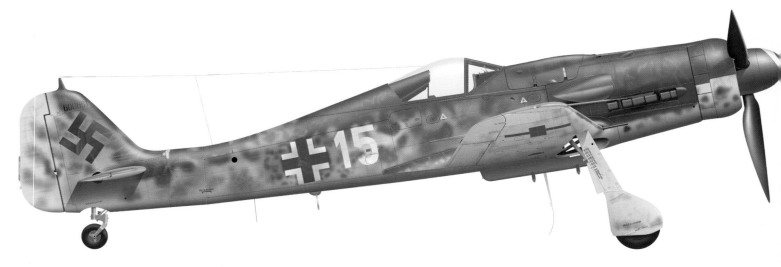

Focke-Wulf Fw 190 D-9, 'White 15', Straubing, 1945

While the hard demarcation line on the forward engine cowling is typical of many Fw 190 D-9s, the mottles on the fuselage sides are considerably heavier and denser and the Balkenkreuz is noticeably smaller than usual. Otherwise, the aircraft has 76 on the undersurfaces but the normal camouflage scheme of 75 and 83 on the uppersurfaces has been darkened with random mottles of 82 which also appear on the lower part of the engine cowling. The spinner was green 70 with a white spiral.

ABOVE AND ABOVE RIGHT: A captured Fw 190 D-9 'White 15' at Straubing, May 1945. This machine, W.Nr. 600651, was built by Fieseler in January 1945 and although the unit to which it belonged is not known for certain, the possibility exists that the machine may once have belonged to 9./JG 54, a Staffel known to have used white tactical numbers without an outline. To offset this supposition, however, is the fact that Straubing airfield did not fall into US hands until late April whereas from February 1945, when this Staffel was redesignated 15./JG 26, most of IV./JG 26's aircraft wore black and white tail bands and a wavy Gruppe bar aft of the Balkenkreuz, neither of which were applied to this machine.

RIGHT: The unit to which this surrendered Fw 190 D-9 belonged is uncertain, although the aircraft's tactical number repeated on the lower undercarriage door is a feature seen on similar machines operated by 7./JG 26. If this supposition is correct, then the aircraft was 'Brown 2', possibly W.Nr. 210022. Note the unusual finish on the undercarriage door of the Fw 190 on the left.

THIS PAGE: Although JG 6 had been allocated red/white/red tail bands, they were not carried by this Fw 190 D-9, 'Black 12' of II./JG 6, which landed on the airfield at Fürth on 8 May 1945 where the pilot gave himself up to US personnel *(ABOVE)*. Tail bands were intended to aid aerial recognition in the daylight battles in the West, whereas when II./JG 6 received the D-9 it was flying tactical operations against Soviet forces in the East and the requirement for them was therefore redundant. An interesting feature of this particular machine, W.Nr. 500570, is the undulating demarcation line between the upper and undersurface fuselage colours. This was typical of aircraft with Werknummern in the 500XXX series.

Focke-Wulf Fw 190 D-9 'Black 12' of II./JG 6, Fürth, 8 May 1945

Most of the fuselage sides on this aircraft were finished in the greenish tinge of 76 which was quite common towards the end of the war. Other parts of the airframe were camouflaged in the much bluer shade of 76, particularly on the undercarriage fairings and rudder. Other interesting features include the 82 on the forward engine cowling, the 83 on the mid-fuselage and the grey 75 on the spine which has been extended to include the very light mottling on the tail. Note also the red primer on the fuselage and under the wings which were largely natural metal with blue-grey 76 being used on the ailerons. Wing and tailplane uppersurfaces were in 75 and 83.

ABOVE: This aircraft dump at Straubing at the end of the war contained an Fw 190 D-9 in the foreground and also at least one Ta 152. The machine nearest to the camera is 'Yellow 15', a wingless Fw 190 D-9, W.Nr. 500666, with the yellow and red fuselage bands of JG 301. The damage to this machine indicates that its last flight ended in a crash-landing with further damage being caused when the aircraft was dismantled and moved to its final resting place. Note, that what appears to be a small horizontal bar on the rear fuselage is thought to have been either a smudge of grime from the lifting hole, and has been shown as such in the accompanying profile, or was a dent or tear in the skin which probably occurred later. Behind 'Yellow 15' and facing in the opposite direction is a Ta 152 H-1, W.Nr. 150167, and although this aircraft had no unit markings it is thought that it, too, was destined for JG 301.

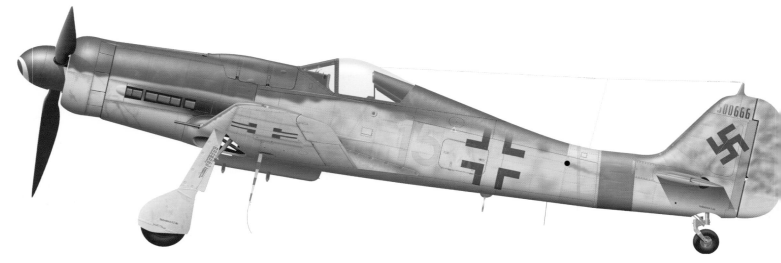

Focke-Wulf Fw 190 D-9 'Yellow 15' of I./JG 301, May 1945
Due to the condition of this machine in the reference photograph, much of this profile is speculative although the camouflage colours were almost certainly 75 and 83 on the uppersurfaces and the usual 76 below. On the fuselage, these colours were separated on the fuselage by a relatively hard, slightly undulating demarcation line. Fuselage mottling was minimal but was denser on the vertical tail surfaces, and the spinner was black-green 70 with a white spiral.

RIGHT: In Jagdwaffe Volume 5, Section 2, the suggestion was put forward that, in the final weeks of the war, a new camouflage scheme may have been introduced which involved light coloured mottles applied over a darker base. On fighter aircraft, this scheme appears to have consisted of various combinations of 75, 81, 82 and 83 mottled with 76, and although the logic of such a scheme was discussed, an inexplicable feature was that, on fighter types, it was only applied to the fuselage. Further examples of this finish are shown here on the fuselage of this Bf 109 G-6, W.Nr. 410061, photographed at Wunstorf in May 1945, and the two Fw 190 D-9s shown opposite.

LEFT: This Fw 190 D-9 coded 'Black 11' was photographed at Bayreuth-Bindlach in the summer of 1945, evidently after making a crash-landing at the end of the war. Although the tail of the aircraft and one of the recognition bands are missing, they were probably black/white/black, indicating that the machine belonged to JG 4. While most of this Geschwader's pilots flew to Flensburg or Leck shortly before the surrender, it is thought that the pilot of this aircraft headed for Bayreuth-Bindlach in order to be nearer his home. The Jumo engines of all Fw 190s were supplied as a complete unit — a so-called 'power egg' —and were delivered with cowlings already painted by the Junkers factory in accordance with prevailing camouflage directives.

RIGHT: Another example of the light mottle over darker colours may be seen on the engine cowling of this Fw 190 D-9 which was photographed at Rhein-Main near Frankfurt in April 1945. The black/white/black bands around the rear fuselage indicate that the aircraft belonged to JG 4 while the Stab markings on the fuselage comprising two horizontal bars and a chevron in black outlined in white suggest that this may have been the aircraft assigned to the Geschwader's last Kommodore, Eichenlaubträger Obstlt. Gerhard Michalski.

Focke-Wulf Fw 190 D-9 of Stab/JG 4, Frankfurt/Main area, April 1945

This machine was fitted with early head armour and an early, unblown canopy. The camouflage finish was 75 and 83 on the uppersurface with undersurfaces in 76, and the engine cowling was mottled with 75. The black/white/black identification bands of JG 4 were applied around the rear fuselage and these were further outlined with a thin white line and an even thinner black edging. The spinner, which was marked with a white spiral, was probably black.

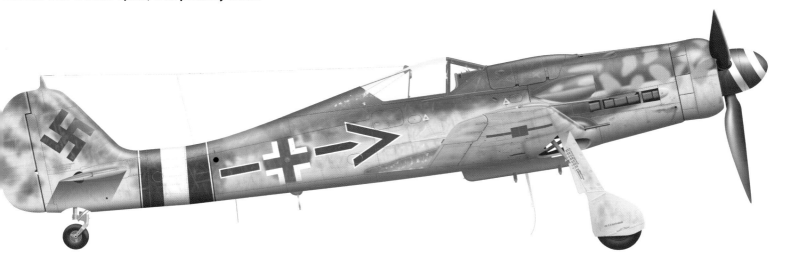

THIS PAGE: This Fw 190 A-8 of the Gruppenstab of I./JG 301 was photographed by American troops of the 6th Armored Division during their advance through Germany in April or May 1945, but the precise location is not known. Note the most simplified style of cross on the fuselage and under the wings and that the engine number, in this instance 339786, has been painted on the lower cowl ring.

Focke-Wulf Fw 190 A-8 of Stab, I./JG 301, Germany, April/May 1945

Although 'Chevron 4' was camouflaged on the fuselage and uppersurfaces in a 74/75/76 scheme which had become largely obsolete in the final months of the war, the undersurfaces of the wings and undercarriage doors were more typical of the period in being only partly painted so that some areas remained in natural metal. All national markings were in the late war austere style and the spinner was plain green 70 with no spiral. Hardly visible in the profile due to shadow is the engine number 339786 on the lower part of the cowl ring. Note the grey 75 on the lower part of the undercarriage fairing.

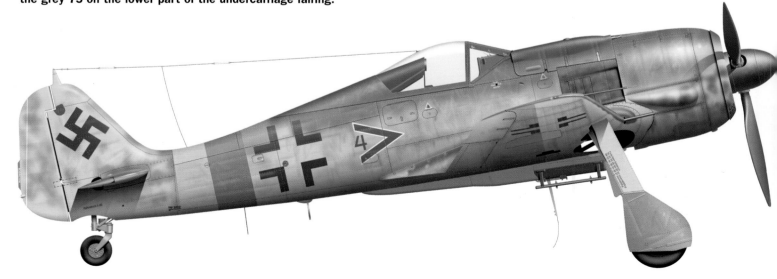

THIS PAGE:
This Fieseler-built Fw 190, W.Nr. 681330, was originally manufactured as an A-8 in the summer of 1944 but was later modified and converted to an F-8 with outer wing cannon deleted and ETC bomb racks added beneath the wings and fuselage. The unit with which the machine flew while in the fighter configuration has not been established, but it is thought that, after being converted to an F-8, it served on the Eastern Front with the ground-attack unit II./SG 2. At the end of the war, the pilot of this aircraft flew to Neubiberg and surrendered to the Americans. Despite the amount of reworking required to convert the aircraft from a fighter to a ground-attack machine, the repainting was very rudimentary, the new camouflage on the fuselage sides barely covering the former fighter markings which consisted of the number '7' and a vertical III. Gruppe bar, both in red with no outline. Once delivered to II./SG 2, the machine was given a new identity and became 'Yellow 11' with a yellow II. Gruppe horizontal bar, both markings being edged in black. Note that, as shown above, although the outer wing guns were removed, the associated wing bulges on the uppersurface of the wings were retained.

Focke-Wulf Fw 190 F-8 'Yellow 11' of II./SG 2, Neubiberg 1945
This machine, W.Nr. 681330, was camouflaged in a 75/83/76 scheme with the rudder and the front of the engine cowling painted yellow. The latter was the result of vague instructions issued on 7 March 1945 to units operating under Luftflotte 4 and which often resulted, as here, in the whole front of the cowling being painted yellow in error instead of having a 500 mm wide yellow band, as was the intention. The spinner markings were in black and white, and although late-war austere type national markings appeared on the fuselage and tail, the crosses under the wings were the black mid-war type with white outlines. Note the rather ineffective attempts to overspray the aircraft's original red fuselage markings.

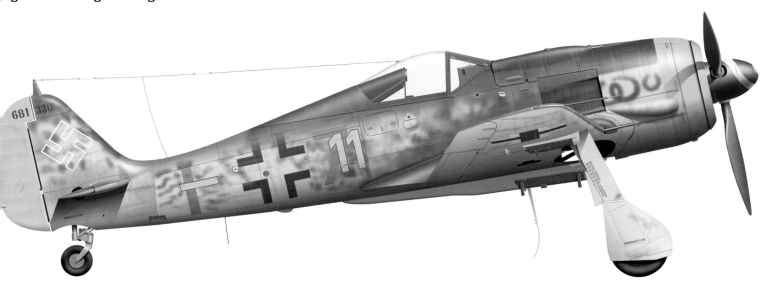

LEFT: This further view of the same 'Yellow 11' shown on the previous page was taken several months later and shows that, once the fuselage camouflage had weathered, the earlier red markings became even more obvious. In the background showing a more concerted attempt to obscure earlier markings, is another Fw 190 F-8, 'Yellow 12', another aircraft from II./SG 2 which probably surrendered at Neubiberg at the same time as 'Yellow 11'. The nose of the Fw 190 A-8 on the right of the picture belonged to W.Nr. 681382 and was flown by Hptm. Wilhelm Moritz, the former Kommandeur of IV./JG 3. A complete view of this aircraft is shown on Page 46.

RIGHT: Null Uhr. This photograph of sheep grazing around a wrecked Fw 190 of the former II./JG 301 could have been taken at Fürth, Langensalza, Braunschardt or, indeed, almost anywhere the units of the Luftwaffe fled in the final days of the war in May 1945 and seems to typify the situation in Germany at that time. The Wehrmacht had been defeated, the nation ceased to exist, foreign armies occupied the ruins of the 'Thousand Year Reich' and for most of the disillusioned and demoralised population that had survived, life was a matter of squalor and hunger. It was – as the Germans themselves called it – 'die Null Uhr', 'Hour Zero'. This was the moment when, as if the hands of a hypothetical stopwatch had been reset, time stood still before ticking towards an uncertain future.

BELOW: The US 6th Armored Division discovered these Fw 190s in the Leina Forest destroyed by retreating German personnel. At least four of the aircraft have completely burned out and although the machine centre left appears to be intact, the rear fuselage has been largely destroyed by flames.